THE
CREATIVITY

D1595144

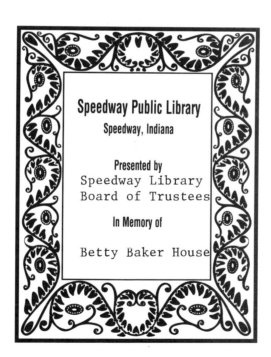

ABOUT THE AUTHOR

Carolyn Boriss-Krimsky, M.A., A.T.R., L.M.H.C., is a visual artist, registered art therapist, licensed mental health counselor, and studio art teacher. She has taught art in universities, mental health centers, public schools, museums, and private studio settings. Ms. Boriss-Krimsky cofounded and codirected a community art gallery and currently directs *Artspace* in Cambridge, Massachusetts, where she conducts private art classes. She has received an award in print-making from the Massachusetts Artists Foundation and is also a published arts writer. Ms. Boriss-Krimsky, the mother of two children, has spent her adult life making art and using it as a vehicle to develop the self-esteem and creative potential of children and adolescents.

THE
CREATIVITY
HANDBOOK

A Visual Arts Guide for Parents and Teachers

CAROLYN BORISS-KRIMSKY

Charles C Thomas
PUBLISHER • LTD.
SPRINGFIELD • ILLINOIS • U.S.A.

Published and Distributed Throughout the World by

CHARLES C THOMAS · PUBLISHER, LTD.
2600 South First Street
Springfield, Illinois 62794-9265

© *1999 by* CHARLES C THOMAS · PUBLISHER, LTD.

ISBN 0-398-06961-1 (cloth)
ISBN 0-398-06962-X (paper)

Library of Congress Catalog Card Number: 99-18109

With THOMAS BOOKS *careful attention is given to all details of manufacturing
and design. It is the Publisher's desire to present books that are satisfactory as to their
physical qualities and artistic possibilities and appropriate for their particular use.*
THOMAS BOOKS *will be true to those laws of quality that assure a good name
and good will.*

Printed in the United States of America
CR-R-3

Library of Congress Cataloging-in-Publication Data

Boriss-Krimsky, Carolyn.
    The creativity handbook : a visual arts guide for parents and
teachers / by Carolyn Boriss-Krimsky.
        p.   cm.
    Includes bibliographical references and index.
    ISBN 0-398-06961-1 (cloth). -- ISBN 0-398-06962-X (paper)
    1. Art--Study and teaching--Activity programs. 2. Creative ability
in children. 3. Creative ability in adolescence. I. Title.
N350.B656   1999
707'.1--dc21
                                                                99-18109
                                                                CIP
                                                                rev.

To my daughter Alyssa and my son Eliot

PREFACE

Watching young children make art, one can only surmise that artmaking comes from a raw and primitive place in the human psyche. Visual language establishes itself with scribbling at about the age of 2, and it is through scribbling that we connect to the written word. The discovery, in 1980, of a Middle-Eastern art object thought to have predated Homo sapiens (250,000 years ago) implies that artmaking may have existed even in prehuman creatures. This finding not only gives credence to the universality and power of artmaking, it also establishes art as having evolutionary origins.

I have often wondered: if art is such a natural part of the human experience (and maybe the prehuman experience), then why, as we get older, does it seem foreign to so many of us? My book attempts to answer that question by describing what authentic art experience is for the child, how developmental changes influence creativity, and what the social and educational forces are that influence the child/adolescent.

In my years of teaching, I have been guided by two ideas that I acquired from my students: Young children instinctively tell the truth about the way they see the world, and they paint their experiences as they feel them. That is one of the reasons that children's art has always been a source of inspiration for visual artists. At various times in their careers, famous painters such as Wassily Kandinsky, Gabriele Münter, Paul Klee, and Pablo Picasso were greatly influenced by children's art. Yet, in our schools and in the home, children's art is hardly cherished or nurtured enough. As children get older, many of them begin to disconnect from artmaking because they fail to receive adult support, and eventually, they lose interest. I believe that children's art gets stultified at an early age by rigid school systems, budget cuts, and ironically, well-meaning parents and teachers who unintentionally turn children away from their own authentic vision.

After working as an art educator and an art therapist for over 20 years, I have seen the way that making art can heal by tapping into the subconscious mind and creating transformational moments for children and adolescents. Through my work in diverse settings such as urban public schools, art museums, mental health centers, and art studios, I have had the opportunity to learn a lot about the lives of my students and to interpret their personal experiences through their artistic creations. I have seen how children and adolescents can gain self-esteem and confidence when their artistic ideas and perceptions are acknowledged and validated by others. But, I have also worked with students who believe that they are unable to create art because parents and teachers have made them feel that they did not have the "skill." I believe that artmaking is much more than a skill and that the potential and the instinct to make art is in all of us. However, parents and teachers need to support that potential so that a context is established where the creative process can unfold and the child's artistic imagination can become fully realized.

The purpose of *The Creativity Handbook* is to demystify art for parents and teachers and to help them understand what the art experience is like for the child/adolescent. The book discusses visual art concepts in simple terms and presents art as a vehicle for educationally transformative experiences. The book also provides sample dialogues between adults and children for parents and teachers who wish to help children approach art projects creatively. The "I can't draw" syndrome is explained and stages of artistic development are discussed from scribbling to adolescent art. *The Creativity Handbook* also offers ideas and projects to help adults support the authentic vision of the child/adolescent throughout all the stages.

In addition, *The Creativity Handbook* presents teachers and educators with ideas for working with students who have unconventional learning styles or who might be considered "behavior problems." Hands-on projects presented in the book can either be modified to fit traditional classroom settings or can be a stimulus for educators to create their own version of art-related projects. By understanding how developmental changes are reflected in artmaking, teachers and educators can be more genuine in their interactions with children and adolescents.

At the core of this book is the belief that children are born artists and that artistic talent emerges from the interplay of proclivity, cultural enrichment, and nurturance. I believe that artmaking is an integral part of the human experience and that its proper role in the child's development is poorly understood. I hope that this book will raise consciousness and foster understanding about the nature of the art experience and that it will help adults find ways to keep the creative process alive at home and in the classroom, not only for their children, but also for themselves.

INTRODUCTION

Writing this book combines two of my greatest loves: art and children. Both have had a profound effect on my life. Besides having children of my own, I have worked with children and adolescents for all of my adult life. I feel very close to my *child-spirit* and much of my inspiration comes from the connection I have to that part of my being. As an artist, I view the universal childhood experience as a rich emotional resource for creative expression.

My recollection of making art when I was a child is that time stood still. There was no need for words. I felt peaceful, almost hypnotized. I lost track of where I was and what was going on around me. There was something powerful, even secret, about it. It was my own experience, one that I couldn't (and didn't want to) share with anyone. At the age of 9, I learned that art could also be healing. By that age, I had developed a stutter which lasted for a few years. Mostly, I would stutter when I had to "perform" in front of people (like read out loud at school). Making art was very reassuring to me because it enabled me to express myself without having to speak. I continued using art as an emotional anchor throughout my adolescence. By that point, I had begun to view art as a dialogue with self, rather than a "skill."

Being a visual artist has provided me with a degree of critical distance from the world, but also with a strong sense of identity, wholeness, and well-being. The creative, intuitive part of myself has pulled me through periods of turmoil, taken me to exotic places (internal and external), kept me company, and allowed me to take chances.

I do not recall what age I was when I heard about *creativity*, but I remember thinking that the word sounded magical. Unfortunately, many school systems are set up in such a way that creativity becomes little more than an abstract concept. For most adults, visual art expression becomes an inaccessible, almost mythical activity that just a few "talented" people can do. This attitude gets passed down through the generations, either at home or at school, and eventually, children start to question the validity of their own image-making.

I wrote this book for caring adults who want to make art accessible to children and adolescents by supporting and validating young people's perceptions of life experiences through the media of the visual arts.

Today, many parents are concerned that their children are spending too much time with computers, video games, TV, and other screen activities. As schools cut back on programs in the arts, parents may feel the need to become more proactive in the creative life of their child. This book offers that opportunity by presenting parents with concrete ways to nurture their child's creativity. Also, educators who want to devise age-appropriate and developmentally relevant art projects as well as those who want to use art more effectively in special-needs programs will benefit from this book. Teachers who battle budget cuts and find themselves (with little or no art education) either teaching art or using it in the course curriculum will be able to use the book as a resource. Art therapists will also be able to use the book as a reference guide for designing art projects for children and adolescents with special problems.

My goal in writing the book will be realized if parents, teachers, special-needs educators, art therapists, and other adults concerned with creative education use its message and projects as an inspiration to help support the authentic vision of the child/adolescent.

ACKNOWLEDGMENTS

I would like to give special acknowledgment to Marcia Yudkin and Denise Bergman whose expert advice and criticism were invaluable to me through various stages of this project. I am grateful to Monona Rossol, Director of Arts, Crafts and Theater Safety in New York City, for her excellent contribution to the Art Materials and Safety Information Appendix and to Mary Jo Clark for her enthusiasm and help with running the art group for younger children. I would also like to thank the following people who generously gave their time to read sections of the book, offered insights, suggestions, and feedback or helped me in other ways: Alicia Faxon, Karen Frostig, Peggy Barnes Lenart, Bette Ann Libby, Kristen Mitchell, and Carol Seitchik.

Since the genesis of this book comes from my deep connection to children, first I want to thank my own children, Alyssa and Eliot, for constantly teaching me to see the world from another perspective. My children were the initial inspiration behind this book because watching them create art and music, write stories, and invent their own ways of doing things added greatly to my fascination with children's creativity.

Next, I would like to thank all of the children and adolescents I taught over the years whose paintings, drawings, and sculptures laid the groundwork for this project. I also want to express my appreciation to my former students who have contributed artwork that appears in the book. They are: Julia Beatty, Leah Levin Beeferman, Walker West Brewer, Carter Doyle, Mel-Jordon Fein, Josh Hartley, Meradith Hoddinott, Matthew Isles, Sarah Jefferson, Emily Kawachi, Zachari Krikorian, Alyssa Krimsky, Eliot Krimsky, Lia Barnes Lenart, Anna Levenson, Eli Levin-Goldstein, Maggie Long, Meghan Mitchell, Annie Karem Oliver-Steinberg, Maria Orlic, Case Randall, Max Razdow, Sarah Reifman-Wheeler, Amanda Salisbury, Justin Sanders, and Garrett Sibinga.

I am very grateful to my mother, Eve Boriss, for all of the educational and artistic opportunities that she provided for me, and to my sister, Barbara Epstein, who always believed in my art. I also want to acknowledge my cousin, Deborah Kraut, for her continued encouragement during this process. Finally, I want to thank my husband, Shelly, for his enduring love and support.

CONTENTS

THE
CREATIVITY
HANDBOOK

Chapter 1
ART EXPERIENCE

WATCHING CHILDREN MAKE ART

For many of us who are convinced that we never knew how to draw and paint, or think we forgot how, it is an awesome experience to watch young children make art. By the time children reach age 2 or so, most of them are happily scribbling on any available surface in the house (frequently, the floor, the table, or the walls). Until the age of 7 or 8, most children continue confidently and enthusiastically painting and drawing, usually on more appropriate surfaces like paper or cardboard. Often a young child can be heard singing or talking to herself as she paints, lost in a world of rich and fanciful images. Sometimes she will tell elaborate stories about real things she has seen or experiences that have inspired the artwork. She will often delight adults with made up stories about anything, even drawings and paintings that consist of only scribbled lines, circles, blobs, or just a few drips of paint.

As we watch children so gloriously lost in the world of creativity and imagination, we sadly realize that eventually, their rich inner-world will be challenged by adult aesthetic standards, and by cultural, developmental, and educational influences. Well-meaning parents and teachers often give feedback that causes children to question the way they represent the world in their paintings and drawings. At what point in their development do children start questioning their artistic ability? What eventually happens to the artist in them and ultimately, in all of us? Does the ability to make art ever really go away? What can we do as parents and educators to keep the creative spirit alive for our children so that they never disconnect from it? This chapter will address these questions and explore some of the ways that children approach artmaking.

THE BEGINNING

Before we go any further, let's start at the beginning, even before a child puts down a mark on paper. Where does artmaking come from and how does it start? According to Viktor Lowenfeld and W. Lambert Brittain, art education pioneers and authors of *Creative and Mental Growth*, the foundation for artmaking begins as soon as the child starts reacting to the world through touching, listening, tasting, and crawling. Children continue to explore their environment through creative play, which eventually leads them into activities such as artmaking.

The very first marks that children make are usually in the form of a scribble. When children (between 18 months and 2 years) gain enough motor control to start scribbling, the experience of mark-making is a surprising and powerful one. In fact, it takes a while for children to realize that the marks being made on paper are actually coming from them.

Once scribblers have gained control over the marks they make, they can change the direction of their arm movements whenever they choose to. Straight, curved, and diagonal lines become repeated and varied. For the curious child, it is not too much of a leap to turn a circle into a face or a squiggle into a worm. When that begins to happen, the child moves from being an instinctive scribbler to a deliberate image-maker. Scribbling also leads the child into written language.

MAKING ART

Any group of random marks on paper can be considered an artistic expression, but what brings it to the level of *art* is an original and adventurous way of putting it all together. The act of artmaking comes out of a combination of conscious and subconscious processes. In order to draw an object, a child has to have a conscious, sensory experience of it. At the same time, the element of subconscious process, such as how the child feels about the subject matter of the drawing, will be an important part of the artwork. For instance, a child who just received a new bicycle has direct knowledge about what the bike looks like. She has not only seen it many times, but she also knows what it feels like to ride it. She may think about it a lot and maybe she even dreams about it.

When she goes away from the bike, she can still picture what it looks like because she has a visual memory of it. She also knows what it's like to fall off the bike, to ride fast on a windy day, and to feel unsteady when the bike gets wobbly. The child may have a mixture of subliminal feelings about the bike, like: it's beautiful, it's exciting, it's big, it's grown-up, and sometimes it's scary. When she creates a drawing of her bike, conscious and subconscious processes will come together and form a work of art that merges developmental, cognitive, and emotional elements.

ART PROCESS

How does art get made? The answer lies in the process the artist went through to make it happen. For the true artist, and the very young child, the product is secondary to the process. Whether a painting emerges out of an art session or not, the experience of creating is what is important, not the actual artwork itself.

Watching the way a preschooler paints is a good example of process-oriented artwork. When a 3- or 4-year-old child makes a painting, it is all about spontaneous experience. Lines are often expressed in quick, sweeping motions, colors are usually dripping and oozing into one another, and shapes may be bold and expressive. If the painting activity stops in a few minutes, it will probably end with an exciting artwork (or product). However, the child may be enjoying the art experience so much that she wants to continue working. If she paints on the same paper, the bold colors and shapes may disappear into a solid mass of brown and muddy goop. Adults who watch the process may be disappointed by the outcome, but the child will be just as happy with the brown blob as she would be with the bold shapes and bright colors. For her, it is not important what the painting looks like in the end. She just knows that she had fun making it.

VISUAL THINKING

In his book *Visual Thinking*, the psychologist Rudolf Arnheim said, "Thinking calls for images and images contain thought."[1] If that is true, then visual thinking is really about the way we perceive and think about the world. By the time we reach adulthood, most of us think about the objective universe in a fairly literal and pragmatic way. Children, on the other hand, see magic and mystery in almost everything they do and see. While adults may be oblivious to such nature-connected phenomena as a sunset turning the sky red, a full moon on a spooky night, or snow falling on a winter day, children will be fascinated, inspired, and curious.

Since young children have a natural inclination to interpret reality, they possess a much more open-ended view of the visual world than adults do. For children, the world looks any way they want it to. Young children's drawings are expressionistic because they are driven by subjective and emotional responses to what they see, feel, and experience. Later, their visual thinking changes as social, cultural, and developmental influences push them toward mastery and correctness.

As adults, the way that we perceive the world has to do with how open we are to new concepts and new ideas. Sometimes, in order to break out of rigid patterns of thinking about things, we need to take our blinders off and begin to *un-see* (or restructure the way we are used to seeing). When we question the "obvious" by thinking in new ways about ordinary experiences, we are connecting to the way young children think and how they see the world.

THE IMAGINATIVE CHILD ARTIST

We have all heard the expression, "In every artist there is a child and in every child there is an artist." This is especially true when the child is between the ages of about 4–7 years old. The artwork that comes after the scribbling stage is often the most innovative work that children produce in their entire lifetime. Somewhere before or around

1. Rudolf Arnheim, *Visual Thinking*. Berkeley: University of California Press, 1969, p.254.

the time that most children enter school, their artistic creativity seems to be highly evolved. Children's early representational attempts are filled with spontaneous, uninhibited, and whimsical images. These drawings are especially moving because the feeling behind them is not only one of excitement and wonder, but also one of complete openness and honesty. Young children are not trying to get anything right or impress anyone. Their drawings reflect their authentic experience, devoid of social norms about how things should be represented.

In looking at a tree, the child may notice its shape, the texture of the bark, the branches, or the leaves. But, she may also have a strong emotional connection to the symbol of a tree. If so, she will project those big feelings onto her visualization. She might have played in a neighbor's tree house or seen a movie about children who were protected by a tree in a snow storm. Perhaps she heard a story about a talking tree, a tree that turned into a monster, or a tree that sprouted gigantic blue flowers. When a 5-year-old child creates an image of a tree, she draws it the way it feels to her and she lets her imagination guide her.

When the child draws mommy and daddy larger than a house, it is because mommy and daddy are so important to her that they *feel* larger than life. With creative abandon that many adult artists yearn to emulate, children at this age will draw a primary shape, and in a matter of seconds, turn it into a polka-dot house, a flying car, a fantastic insect, or a scary monster. A person can "swim" in the sky, be taller than the tallest tree, or fit inside a sunflower. During this wondrous stage and beyond, adults should encourage the child to continue using her imagination and to think of it as a wellspring of ideas that she can always tap into.

The emotional references that young children have, and the fact that they approach the world in an uninhibited and original way, is part of what makes up the dynamic of their artwork. Conventional adult standards of aesthetics and "right" and "wrong" ways of thinking about image-making can only have a negative impact on the raw energy behind children's art. Adults should not be too literal-minded when reacting to the artwork of the imaginative child. It is best to ask a child to talk about her drawings before projecting adult ideas or comments.

THE CONNECTION BETWEEN THE CHILD
AND THE ADULT ARTIST

In his book *Art, Mind and Brain,* developmental psychologist Howard Gardner explores the connections between young children and adult artists. "While mature artists have much better developed skills, far more control of their gifts, and superior abilities to experiment systematically and to choose deliberately among alternatives, much in their processes of creation is reminiscent of children."[2] Gardner notes that the child and the adult artist both explore and mix various art media, both experiment with color, both create symbols that relate to their own expressive need, and both allow play and spontaneity to become an important part of the process. Moreover, both the adult artist and the child transcend conventional boundaries about how things should look, what an artist is supposed to do, or what visual expression should mean. Both are making art because they have a strong need for self-expression. One important difference between the two might be that most adult artists are self-aware and reflective about some aspects of their process, whereas children are not.

Many artists have been fascinated by the spontaneity and vitality behind children's art. In his book *The Innocent Eye,* Jonathan Fineberg chronicles famous artists who not only found inspiration in children's art but also used it as source material for their own work. Among them were Paul Klee, Wassily Kandinsky, Gabriele Münter, and Pablo Picasso. When Paul Klee discovered his childhood drawings one day at his home in Switzerland, he considered it to be one of the most important events of his life. In fact, these drawings became the impetus for some of his later paintings, many of which were considered to be masterpieces. Kandinsky and Münter also collected children's art and used it to search for a visual language that connected to the pure vision of the child. Picasso, on the other hand, was more interested in how children made art than in the products they created. He made careful observations of children at play and became intrigued by their appropriation of objects. (Children who see an opened umbrella may use it in fantasy play as a house.) The concept of appropriation is illustrated in Picasso's sculptures from the early 1950s, where children's toys and other objects are playfully and symbolically used.

---

2. Howard Gardner, *Art, Mind and Brain.* New York: Basic Books, 1982, p.102.

TEACHING ART TO CHILDREN

Although I have been teaching art to children for over twenty years, I consider the term "art teacher" to be an oxymoron, or at least a misnomer. The term "art facilitator" fits more into what experienced art educators do, because I don't believe that art can ever really be taught. I distinguish between the teaching of technical skills or aesthetic principles and actually teaching another human being to find her/his creative center. Finding one's own creative center (or intuitive voice) is something that individuals must accomplish on their own. There is no right or wrong way to do it, nor is there any designated time for it to happen. Since I believe that the creative, intuitive voice has its roots in childhood, it is always within us. But in order to reclaim and develop it, most of us need to go through an ongoing process of introspection and self-discovery.

The irony of the notion of *teaching art to children* is that children already know how to create art. Some of them have just lost touch with it. What I mean is that children come into the world with everything they need to be artists. They spend their whole day pretending, playing, questioning, exploring, and creating. Most children scribble until they are about 3 or 4 years old. At the point when they begin to name their scribbles, and images start to emerge, they have sufficient control over their motor skills to begin a lifetime of creative expression. So, what happens to impede the process?

The reasons that some children begin to lose touch with creative artmaking within the first few years of elementary school, have to do with educational and social systems, parental and peer group influences, and some normal developmental changes that pull children away from the kind of free expression that they exhibited when they were younger. After the ages of 7 or 8, many children look as if they have lost their ability to make free-flowing and spontaneous works of art. Most children at this age really want to do things "right." Developmentally, they're entering a more literal stage, driven by precision and correctness. Learning to read, acquiring math skills, and following school rules feeds into a "right" and "wrong" sensibility that spills over into artmaking. (More on this in Chapter 3.) Getting things "right" may mean for some children that creative image-making is held off for a while, perhaps until they enter or pass through adolescence.

Throughout all of the stages of artistic development that children go through, I believe that something can be reclaimed from the earlier, less literal period. While the artist part of the child's persona may go underground for awhile, and maybe even remain latent into adulthood, it can always be rediscovered. Parents and teachers have the most important role in establishing the nurturance and sense of safety that children need to retain their self-confidence and inner spirit. To a certain extent, original and authentic artwork comes out of a belief in oneself. At some point in the child's development, that belief needs to be fostered by a caring adult.

HELPING THE DEVELOPING CHILD ARTIST

Many art educators believe that children are essentially self-taught artists until about the age of 6 or 7. Around that time (or earlier), cultural factors begin affecting the child's choice of subject matter and even the direction of her art. The influence of parents and other adults on the art of the preschool child may be indirect, but it is very significant. How we respond or don't respond to early scribbles or whether we put our children's artwork up on the wall are some of the ways that we influence children's art. Also, whether or not we provide art materials for the child or give her coloring books (and tell her to color within the lines) may also have an impact on the way the child approaches artmaking. But it is not just coloring books that affect the images that children make. Other cultural influences such as computer games, pictures in children's books, paintings hanging in the home, videos, magazines, movies, and comic books all present the child with pre-set formulas for representing objects.

Given all of these factors, how can we best help the developing child continue making expressive artwork and stay connected to creative exploration? The adult can best help the developing child by being a catalyst, a facilitator, an observer, and a friend. It is very important for the adult to provide a stimulating, secure, and loving environment where creative activity can unfold. But at the same time, we need to give the child room for her creative process to develop naturally, without adult interference. Most importantly, we should never try to change the child's original imagery or make her feel inadequate for creating something that we do not understand or recognize. Since art cannot really be technically "taught," adults should avoid showing children how to make visual images. When adults try to manipulate the way a child draws, the child will either use the adult's image a few times and forget it (a good move on her part, if she can pull it off) or she may think about it too much and let the adult image dominate her work.

Children are astute observers of the world and they make art out of experiences that are important to them in their own lives. Most adult imagery is usually stereotypic and rigid, and, even if it were wildly inventive, it still has nothing to do with how the child sees and connects to the world. If an adult shows a child how to make an object such as a boat, every time that child draws a boat, she is thinking "right" and "wrong." She may be forgetting her own experience of being on a boat because she is so busy remembering and trying to copy the adult version she has just learned.

If a child says, "Show me how to draw a boat," the adult can say something like, "If I show you how to draw a boat, you may think my drawing is right and yours is wrong. But there is no right or wrong way to make art. Your drawing is special because it comes from you, not me."

At that point, the adult can try to help the child recreate a memorable time that she had recently when she went on a boat ride. The following questions may allow the child to reclaim the moment, "Remember the last time we went to the lake? We were all in the motorboat and you watched me catch a fish, right? Can you remember what it felt like when we were gliding in the water? How many people did we have in the boat? Can you remember the colors of the boat? Did it feel bumpy when the boat went fast?"

This kind of interaction helps put the child back in control of her own experience. She is an expert on her life, even at a young age. When she remembers what it was like to be on the boat that day and how she felt about it, her visualization will reflect authentic experience.

The child will feel even more empowered if some of her artwork is framed and exhibited in a prominent place in the home. When children see their work hanging in their homes, next to adult artwork, they know they are being taken seriously.

The next chapter looks at various aspects of creativity, including cultural misconceptions and myths that effect the developing child.

Chapter 2
CREATIVITY AND THE CHILD

This chapter explores the concept of creativity and looks at some popular beliefs that surround it. What is the meaning of *talent* and what relationship does it have to creativity? What is the connection between children and creativity? The following myths reveal commonly held cultural misconceptions that can have a profound effect on the child's artistic self-confidence.

Artists Are Born, Not Made.

This myth seems to imply that artmaking is a magical skill that only a select group of people possess. The ability to create art is sometimes viewed as an inherited trait, like having blue eyes. Nothing could be further from the truth. I believe that the skills we need to make art can be acquired by anyone interested in learning them. The skills are nothing more than practical tools needed to expand and develop a visual vocabulary. Just as mathematicians often use numerical formulas to solve problems, visual artists work with various media so that they can broaden their range of expression.

I believe that artists are born *and* made. All of us are born artists in the sense that we have inherent potential and a primitive impulse to make art. From the moment that we first grab a crayon and start scribbling on tables, the walls, or the floor, we are connecting to a primordial need that was shared by the earliest human creatures who existed tens of thousands of years ago. Prehistoric cave paintings have shown us that art was the first form of recorded communication. The existence of these paintings proves that art is a timeless, universal language that connects the present to our past and our future. But, if the language of art is so universal and the urge to create it is so ingrained into the fabric of human experience, then why do so many of us disconnect from it? One reason is that art has lost its functional role in contemporary society. In tribal cultures, art objects such as masks and statues play a part in ritualistic ceremonies that are meant to heal the sick, scare away evil spirits, and protect people from harm. In modern technological society, art has become detached from ordinary people's lives while its products have become objects of status and financial investment. As a culture, we don't consciously view art as something healing, or something that we need emotionally or psychologically in order to survive. Yet children carry the legacy of our ancient ancestors by acting out the impulse to make art, even without much social reinforcement.

Because most young children are still excited about making art, our role as adults should be to sustain that excitement. Many of us, as parents and teachers, remember negative educational experiences that hampered our self-expression and made us question our abilities. But, regardless of our past, or maybe because of it, we want to make art a positive experience for our children. However, if the artist is going to be *made*, we need to let the child develop artistically in his own way. Parents and teachers should provide the art materials, the place where artmaking can happen, lots of stimulation and, of course, emotional support. But, art cannot be reaffirming for children if we impose our personal expectations and values on their artwork. All children's paintings will not be beautiful, colorful, and cheerful, and they shouldn't be. Sometimes it is the messy, muddy, and frenetic-looking paintings that have the most meaning for the child. We must remember that artmaking is more about process than it is about product. Ideally, our children should be making art because they need to express their innermost thoughts, feelings, and perceptions about the world, and not because they want to please us.

Only Talented People Can Draw.

We have all admired the skills of people who are considered exceptional or talented. Regardless of whether they are involved in academics, sports, computer technology, or the arts, talented people just seem to have a special capacity for doing things better than most of us can. But where does this special ability come from? No one knows for sure, but it is thought that we come into the world with certain innate proclivities, like being able to run fast or having a beautiful singing voice. These talents ebb and flow, depending on a variety of factors like the family support system and other cultural, social, and educational influences. In a book called *Talented Teenagers* by Csikszentmihalyi, Rathunde, and Whalen, the concept of talent is defined as "a process that unfolds over many years rather than a trait that one inherits and then keeps unchanged for the rest of life."[3] Many of us think of talented people as luckier than we are because they seem assured of easy success. But, sadly, according to the authors, talent seldom fulfills its promise, not because of lack of skill, but because social realities constrain opportunities. Talent requires a favorable social climate, a viable market for the skill, and pure luck (and lots of it) if it is to be fully realized.

When we were in school, many of us heard the expression, "Only talented people can draw." If we were sitting next to someone in art class who could draw a still life with an exquisite realistic quality, we probably had a very envious reaction. We might have wondered, "What's the point? Why should I even attempt to draw anything when people like this can do it so much better than I can?" We may have been too intimidated to even try. But, because of that, we might have lost an opportunity to learn something. We can be respectful of other people's talent, and yet, not let it stand in our way. The following reasons explain why we should encourage our children to try anyway:

1. Everyone's vision is different, unique, and valid. Making art is not a contest. Evaluating the products of art is a highly subjective matter and should be irrelevant to the act of creating.

2. If talent is a process, that means it can grow and develop. We are not always aware of all of our talents because we may not have had opportunities to try them all out.

3. Regardless of the outcome (or product), artmaking is an experience that is, in itself, worth having.

4. Art remains a multilayered process that goes beyond goal orientation. Each time we make art, we don't know what is going to happen or how we are going to feel about it. For some children and adolescents, depending on their developmental level and their particular

3. Mihaly Csikszentmihalyi, Kevin Rathunde, Samuel Whalen, *Talented Teenagers*, New York: Cambridge University Press, 1993, p.26.

way of looking at the world, artmaking may be about capturing a time, place, or event. For others, artmaking may be less about depicting an objective universe and more about expressing concepts, ideas, emotions, and feelings. But regardless of what we thought art was about when we originally made it, it may take on new meaning years after it is created.

5. Creativity and talent are not the same thing, although they are mutually reinforcing. Talent may be expressed in the way that a person technically renders the drawing, but creativity is the vision that brings a piece together in a unique way. Often the artwork of the creative person, even if he is not technically skilled, is far more dynamic and interesting than the work of the more talented individual who may produce artwork that is competent but unimaginative.

If You Don't Know How To Draw When You're Young, You'll Never Learn.

This myth makes no sense because drawing is a teachable skill that can be picked up at any time in the life cycle. There is no right or wrong time to become involved in art. People who draw when they are young may not continue and people who felt that they couldn't draw as children could easily end up as creative adult artists. The skill of drawing is not so much a result of what happens at our fingertips, but of what goes on in the visual centers of our brains.

In her book *Drawing on the Right Side of the Brain*, Betty Edwards states that if we rethink the way we see, we might have less trouble with the way we draw. After looking at research studies on the human brain, Edwards realized that, in order to draw, we have to shift from a verbal or analytical way of processing visual information (left brain) to a more global or intuitive way (right brain). The book chronicles Edwards's work with adults, many of whom had stopped drawing when they were young and were convinced that they could never learn. By creating original and well-thought-out teaching methods and backing them up with established theories about the brain and visual perception, Edwards has exposed the mystique of drawing and taken it away from the myth of the "talented" artist. Because of the work she has done, hundreds of thousands of people have learned how to draw.

My Child Can't Draw a Straight Line.

I have often heard parents say, "My child can't draw a straight line." (My response is usually, "Good, who would want to?") The implication of the straight line remark is that the parent suspects that the child does not have the "talent" that he needs to create the adult version of *good* artwork. These kinds of comments, especially if overheard by the child, can be very harmful. We need to think carefully about what we say to children (and what we say in front of them). I once overheard a parent, who, after looking at her child's drawing, said something like, "Don't worry dear, not everyone can draw." Comments like this can really hurt the child's self-esteem. Since adults are authority figures for children, when we say something bad about them, they interpret it as the absolute truth. The child who was just told that he cannot draw may feel that on a certain level he has already "failed." He may be convinced that he should not even try to make art, because he has already been told by an adult that he is not good at it. Once we understand that making art is a process that consists of much more than just drawing skills, then we have freed ourselves of a constraining myth that dampens the child's motivation to develop his own unique visual language.

My Child Is Just Not Creative.

I have never met a child who is not creative. Creativity and childhood are practically synonymous (see the section in this chapter on Creativity and Childhood). I suspect that people who think of their children as not being creative also see themselves like that. Those who think they are not creative usually have that view of themselves because, in the past, someone made them feel that way. Often, it was an important adult whom they looked up to when they were young. The idea that we are not "good" at art gets planted in many of us when we enter elementary school and come in contact with unimaginative teachers who make us feel that there is only one way to draw things. It is no surprise that, some time after entering elementary school, many of us fall into the "I can't draw" syndrome. The syndrome essentially means, "I can't draw the way I think I'm supposed to, so I guess I can't draw at all." Before entering elementary school, most children are happily drawing and painting without worrying about what other people think of their work. But as soon as they begin to draw more realistically (after about age 7), many children start becoming self-conscious. During the transition from spontaneous art expression to a more literal interpretation of the world, some of them may lose confidence and begin to see themselves as artistically unskilled. Although skill and creativity are different, many of us erroneously believe that if we think of ourselves as being artistically unskilled, then we are also uncreative.

Some Children Are Better at Art than Others.

When I hear people say that some children are better at art than others, I wonder if they mean simply that some children draw more realistically than others do. I also suspect that the word "better" is being used incorrectly. Maybe what they really mean is that some children express themselves in ways that appeal to us more than others do. We feel comfortable with images that we know, and we like looking at paintings where familiar images appear. It follows that some of us would encourage our children and adolescents to draw objects in a realistic way because that is what we think good artists do. Many of us believe that good, and certainly great, artists are more than proficient at drawing anything from landscapes to the figure. Although we think that artists must be highly skilled in basic drawing techniques (and that includes the rendering of "correct" proportion, modelling, and three-dimensional space), this is not always true. One of the most innovative and internationally acclaimed abstract painters, Frank Stella, publicly stated that he does not have conventional drawing skills.[4] This self-proclaimed lack of ability to draw has hardly hampered his enormous creative output and the effect he has had, not only on the art world, but also on a public audience.

Stella, perhaps inadvertently, may have opened up the floodgates of this topic and gotten a lot of people thinking about the intersection between certain kinds of technical skills and the broader issue of creativity. The first thing we have to realize is that drawing is only one kind of skill in art. Painting, printmaking, sculpture, ceramics, video, collage, multimedia, and computer-generated work are forms of visual expression that involve many other kinds of skills. Some creative

---

4. Personal communication with Frank Stella, Tufts University, February 24, 1998.

people are simply not interested in learning and mastering certain kinds of techniques, such as those involved in realistic drawing, because they may find them too rigid or boring, too much of an end in themselves, or simply too hard to learn. Creativity doesn't follow any order of proficiencies. We do not have to master the technical discipline of drawing before we can start to paint. As parents and teachers, we should let go of self-imposed constraints and support whatever creative expression feels right for our children. Sometimes one art form won't work for the child, while another will.

As a teenage art student, I remember taking a pottery class that focused exclusively on using a potter's wheel. (The idea is to make a pot out of a mound of clay while it is spinning on a rotating base.) I found this very difficult and was never able to create anything even vaguely resembling a pot. Most of my clay attempts eventually cracked, fell, or broke apart. To my dismay, I stood out as the worst in the class and was publicly admonished by the teacher for my lack of skills. I frequently asked the instructor if I could make a pot by hand and just avoid the wheel altogether, but he insisted that I could not. If I had let him, that insensitive teacher could have made me feel incompetent, not just about throwing a pot, but about my art ability in general. It is easy for some authoritative and unenlightened adults to make children and adolescents feel like failures. As parents and teachers, we should try to be aware of such situations and help our children weather these kinds of negative educational experiences.

All children have different ways of expressing themselves and they should be encouraged to work in the style and form that is most natural for them. In *Creative and Mental Growth*, Lowenfeld and Brittain distinguish two basic types of creative expression that are observable after a child reaches about the age of 12. They are categorized as *haptic* and *visual*. The haptic type of person is thought to be more emotional, and more subjective while the visual type of person is considered to be more distant, and more of an observer. The haptic type experiences the world physically and intuitively. Colors are bright, shapes are bold, and distorted images are used to express an idea or a feeling. The visual type of person, on the other hand, thinks about the outward appearance of things and is more concerned with objective reality. Paintings are realistically oriented and proportion, depth, and perspective are emphasized. Few of us fit exclusively into one category or the other. Some of us respond to our experiences with more haptic imagery (subjective) and others respond with more visual imagery (objective). These forms of expression should never be critically compared. Children who favor one type over another are not better at art.

Creativity and Childhood

Creativity is a concept that eludes a simple definition. There are many ways to think about it. According to Teresa Amabile, a specialist in creativity, creativity is a combination of imaginative thinking skills, expertise in a particular area, and a passion. In their book *The Creative Spirit*, Goleman, Kaufman, and Ray state that early fascination with a specific activity helps the child develop skills that build mastery and lead the way to a creative life. In Chapter 1, we looked at the similarities and the differences between the child and the adult artist. Now let us look at why so many visual artists, musicians, actors, writers, poets, and other creative souls, refer to their childhood, whether it was a time of happiness or despair, as the wellspring of creativity and the place to return to for ideas and inspiration.

Children are always inventing things; they are naturally creative. Not yet caught up in societal mores, values, traditions, restrictions, and expectations, children are free to ask the basic (and not so simple) questions of life, such as "Can the sun ever fall out of the sky?" or "Why do we grow old?" or "Where do we go after we die?" Creative individuals are people who are able to get back to that magical place of childhood where, ideally, no question is out of bounds and the sense of wonder and excitement about the world is very much alive. What really drives visual artists and other creative people in music, dramatic arts, writing, science, or any other field, is the search for something new and unknown. Often, what feeds that sense of discovery and wonder is *play*, an activity that is intrinsically connected to childhood. Therefore, when thinking about creativity and the creative process, we need to look carefully at young children and the way they approach the world.

When children are playing, they are learning through a discovery process that involves experimenting with new ways of doing things and asking questions. Anyone who has watched a toddler play with simple materials such as a cooking pot and a mixing spoon can't help but be amazed by how much the child can do with simple objects.

First, the child might put the pot on his head to make a hat. Then he might take it off, put it on the ground and use it as a musical instrument, banging on it like a drum. Later, he may turn it upside down and use it as a stool to reach up to get something. Once he has what he needs, he may use the pot as a stage for his stuffed animals. The "stage" may then be turned sideways to become a miniature cave or anything else he wants it to be. Finally, the child may decide that he wants to use the pot to cook with so that he can pretend to be the chef in his favorite restaurant. What makes this so energizing is that the child's ideas keep expanding. Although he might have frequently seen someone use the pot for cooking, he is not limited by the notion that the pot can only be used for one thing. Therefore, he is still able to conjure up new and exciting ways to think about it and, for that matter, anything else that he comes in contact with. For the child, the pot has an infinite variety of possibilities, limited only by his imagination.

Just as creativity is nurtured by new ways of seeing, it is also fed by spontaneity. Both children's play and other forms of creative activities involve the engagement of spontaneous process for its own sake. Although the child may have a desire or a fantasy that initially generates the play, there is usually not a fixed goal or a motive associated with it. A young child will spend long periods of time building expansive structures with blocks because he wants to see what will happen next, not because he will get a reward for building the highest tower. No matter where imaginative children go (especially when there are no conventional toys available), they usually find intriguing things to do. A child playing outdoors might pick up a stick and begin making marks in the dirt. Circles, squares, and squiggle shapes may remind the child of dinosaurs, lizards, or giraffes. Later, he might want to draw other kinds of animals on paper or work with clay or play dough to create an army of pretend creatures from another planet. Working in three dimensions may lead him into dramatic play where he dresses up as a medieval knight, and battles dragons. The child is letting one idea lead him to another. He doesn't start out with a fixed notion of what to do, or follow a formula for how to do it. It is vital that parents and teachers allow this natural process to unfold.

By providing environments that stimulate the child to ask limitless questions and by admitting that we do not have all the answers, we are providing a context for creative discovery to unfold. During the creative process, both the adult artist and the inquisitive child are pursuing an internal quest, even if it is often undefined. The job of searching leads to more experimentation and risk-taking, which are really just grown-up forms of play. In a book called *Creativity*, by Mihaly Csikszentmihalyi, the author found that what drove adults to spend hours on avocations that reaped no eternal gain was the same motivation that we see in children's play: *novelty* and *discovery*. He refers to the feeling of having an optimum enjoyable experience or becoming totally focused on something as *flow*.

When we see children intensely engaged in solitary pursuits such as playing an instrument, reading, drawing, building things, or solving puzzles, we are witnessing a flow state of consciousness where nothing matters but the activity at hand. These extended states of concentrated attention are very important for the child's development. Not only is a lot of cognitive growth occurring, but children get a chance to wind down and take a much needed time-out from social activity. When this special time is nurtured and respected by caring adults, it can grow and become more self-generating. One of the ways we can provide more opportunities for children to experience this kind of internal, sustained focus and enjoyment is to provide constructive and age-appropriate art experiences for them. But, before we explore that, we need to understand the stages of artistic development that children/adolescents go through. The following chapter presents the stages from ages 2 to 17.

Chapter 3
STAGES OF ARTISTIC DEVELOPMENT

FROM SCRIBBLERS TO ADOLESCENT ARTISTS

Creativity is such a complex phenomenon that it is somewhat artificial to reduce it to neat and structured categories. However, for the purpose of this book, creativity in the visual arts will be viewed from the lens of specific developmental stages that children go through from ages 2 to 17. Although the last stage of artistic development covered in this book ends with adolescence, adulthood is a time for many people to explore and reclaim the creativity that was their birthright. The creativity that was so accessible to us as children may fade for a while, but it doesn't permanently disappear. Therefore, it is never too late to regain access to it by exploring the visual arts or, for that matter, any other art form.

Before we look at the stages of artistic development, it should be noted that I am using these stages only as a guide to help us better understand our children's artwork. They are not meant to be used as diagnostic criteria for what is "normal." Stages of artistic development should be viewed as fluid and dynamic, and not as static and rigid. Sometimes children do not fit neatly into each stage at approximately the "correct" age. The developmental stages, defined in this book, as conceived by Viktor Lowenfeld and W. Lambert Brittain (and originally presented in *Creative and Mental Growth*), use the "average" child as a model for growth. But since "average" is an abstraction, we should be aware that some children may be doing artwork that seems age-appropriate, while others may not. My experience with my own children and with students I have taught for over twenty years has shown me that children's artwork can easily extend across more than one stage at the same time. When we talk about creativity and children, there are no hard and fast rules.

According to Lowenfeld and Brittain, the following 6 distinct stages of artistic development define the child's creative growth from ages 2 to 17. Throughout different sections of the book, I use the stages as a basic structure to explore and interpret children's visual art expression and as a way to present some of my own ideas and observations about children's creativity. I also use the stages as a framework to provide age-appropriate art projects for children and adolescents and to illustrate their development through their own artwork.

THE STAGES OF ARTISTIC DEVELOPMENT

The Scribbling Stage (2-4): The child moves from pure processing and exploration to relating scribbles to things in the environment.

The Preschematic Stage (4-7): The child continues to focus on the process of making art as she searches for a way to draw objects. Her artwork expresses what she honestly thinks and feels about a subject.

The Schematic Stage (7-9): The child moves away from focusing on the process of making art and starts thinking about what he is producing. He develops a way of depicting forms and then repeats it again and again. Drawings reflect what the child knows, not what he feels.

The Dawning Realist Stage (9-12): The older child is interested in details and precision. Drawings are product-oriented and reflect the child's conception or characterization of the world rather than a naturalistic depiction of objects.

The Pseudo-Naturalist Stage (12-14): The young adolescent is still product-oriented and is now interested in drawing from nature (especially the human body). She may also be creating fantasy cartoons, doodles, and satirical and exaggerated characters.

Adolescent Art (14-17): The artwork of the older adolescent reflects a search for self. His work involves creative decision-making and experimentation with different techniques, styles, and media. He may focus more on the process of making art than on the product itself.

The Scribbling Stage (2 or Younger–4 Years Old)

The first few years of life establish a crucial foundation for the emotional, psychological, and cognitive development of the child. This is a very exciting period of time because the child is learning language, gaining motor control, exploring the world at breakneck speed, and developing a sense of self. At the beginning of the *Scribbling Stage*, the child has a very short attention span, is distracted easily, and doesn't like to share her toys. She can often be heard saying "No" or asking "Why?" When 2-year-olds gather in a group, they play side by side rather than together. But, by the time the child is three or four, she has an easier time sharing and, to some extent, she has begun to play cooperatively with other children. Throughout many of the early developmental changes that the child goes through, scribbling is a consistent activity for her. As soon as she can physically hold a crayon in her hand, she starts *playing* on paper. The evolution of that play provides us with a precious record of the child's expanding universe.

Scribbling is a natural part of early human behavior that involves processing, playing, and manipulating. It comes about by accident as the child explores and discovers new things in the environment. The moment that a child grabs an object and makes a deliberate mark on a surface, she has started scribbling. Around the time that the child first begins to use crayons and other kinds of drawing tools, she is not fully aware that the marks being made on paper are coming from her. She may not even look at her paper while she scribbles. As the child is busily making marks, lines may be drawn off the sides of the paper, onto the floor or any other surface. But even before she realizes that the marks being made are actually coming from her, she enjoys scribbling because she likes to make big sweeping movements with her hands and arms. The direction, size, and scope of these lines relate to the child's physical size and the development of her motor skills. When children start out scribbling, they are not attempting to draw anything in particular. They are just making marks and exploring what can happen when they move a crayon in one direction or another. The marks they make are as natural to the development of the very young child as walking and talking.

Most adults don't know much about scribbles, except that they seem to be all over the house. Ironically, not knowing much about this mysterious process may not be such a bad thing. According to Rhoda

Kellogg, author of *Analyzing Children's Art,* if we understood more about scribbling, some of us might try to manipulate it and turn it into an adult version of what "art" should be. So long as the child is not scribbling on the walls or on a new kitchen table, we should leave her alone to scribble happily on paper without interference. Often, we look hastily at these scribbles and we don't fully appreciate how much they have developed over time. But a lot is going on for the child. These scribbles reflect how much the child is learning about the world and how her thinking is changing.

Scribbles evolve from being *random* (whatever happens on the page), to *controlled* (the child recognizes that she can control the marks), to *named* (the child connects the marks she makes to something in the environment and then attaches a name to the objects that she recognizes). To understand what the scribbler is really getting at, it can be helpful to look at these progressions more carefully.

Random Scribbles. Early scribble drawings are self-taught, haphazard markings that children seem driven to create. Besides being important in and of themselves, these random scribbles set the stage for future drawing and writing. The child makes accidental and tentative lines that vary in length, shape, size, and direction. Because most early scribblers haven't yet developed fine muscle control, they will use whole arm movements to make large sweeping motions with a crayon or any other drawing tool they can find. If the child is looking away from her paper as she is scribbling, it is probably because she is still not clear where the marks are coming from. Once she figures out that she is the one making all the marks, she scribbles with even more enthusiasm and makes bigger and more expansive gestures than she did before (see Figure 1).

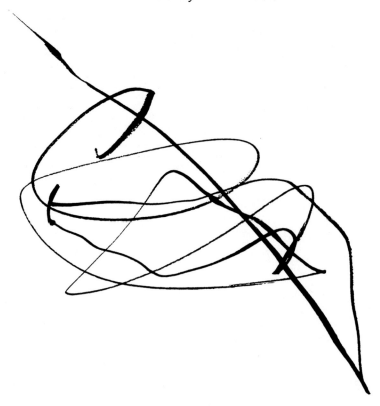

*Figure 1 - **Scribblers:*** Random Scribble by a 22-month-old child. Although this child is playing with making lines and moving her hands in different directions, she may be unaware that she has actually made a scribble. Developmentally, she may not be able to comprehend that she was responsible for making the marks on paper.

Controlled Scribbles. The controlled scribbler already knows that the marks being made on paper are being made by her. She wants to see what will happen when she tries making different kinds of marks and squiggles. Using repeated motions, the child can make distinctive diagonal, horizontal, and vertical lines as well as big and small circle shapes. We may also see the child making dots because, after much experimentation, she has figured out that she can make these kinds of marks by moving the crayon on and off the page. Unlike the random stage where the child is not totally aware of the marks she is making, now she intensely watches her scribbles. While she has better visual and motor control over her scribbles, she is still not consciously replicating anything. As her drawings become more elaborate, she will now spend twice as long scribbling (see Figure 2).

*Figure 2 - **Scribblers**:* Controlled Scribble by a 2-year-old child. This child has discovered that she is in control of the lines being made on paper. She has figured out that if she moves her arm in a certain direction, she can make circular marks with a drawing tool. If she doesn't have crayons or pens around, she might try to make lines and shapes outside in the dirt, the sand, the snow, or the air using a stick or her finger.

Named Scribbles. The child starts naming her scribbles after she has figured out that the shapes she has made look like real objects in the world. The drawings won't change that much, but the child's thinking is different. As she begins a drawing, the child may have a purpose in mind, although this often changes as the drawing evolves. For instance, the child may begin scribbling with the intention of drawing a person. She may say, "I'm going to draw mommy," but just as she makes a mark on paper, something might make her change her mind. The original idea (the "mommy" drawing, in this case) stays open-ended. The child, like most adult artists, doesn't really know what the outcome of the drawing will be. The final image is influenced by the spontaneity of the marks and the connections the child makes to the world around her. If she draws a circle, with the intention of drawing mommy's head, and then suddenly hears someone talking about apples, she may change the direction of her picture and decide to call it "apples" instead. As the child's attention span lengthens, the amount of time that she spends on her drawings increases (see Figure 3).

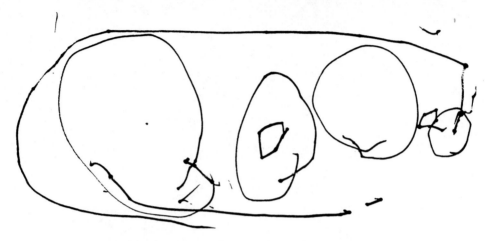

*Figure 3 - **Scribblers***: Named Scribble by a 3¹/₂-year-old child. Once this child discovered that she could make round and oval shapes, she spent a lot of time making them big, small, and in between. While she was scribbling in play group one day, she heard one of the other children tell a story about roller skates. Right after that, she named her scribble "Roller Skate." But, it is not clear that the child actually connected the shapes in her drawing with the visual image of a roller skate. She may have just randomly associated the words with her scribble. Young children will often invent subject matter for their non-representational pictures.

All scribbles consist of different configurations and combinations of dots, lines, loops, and round shapes. Eventually, scribblers make crosses, squares, rectangles, triangles, irregular shapes, and variations of circles. Circular scribblings play an important role in helping the child to move from abstraction to representation. The *mandala* (Sanskrit for circle) is particularly important and intriguing because while it is a religious and mystical symbol dating back to paleolithic times, its origins lie in human scribble movements. The mandala leads to a sun form and eventually to the concept of a person (see Figure 4).

*Figure 4 - **Scribblers/Preschematics**:* Drawing by a 3-year-old child. This early family portrait emerged out of the child's previous scribbling experience, which included making
the universal mandala shape. The mandala led to a sun form (a circle with radiating lines)
and then, over a period of time, to a person. These kinds of radiating lines can become
first the sun's rays and then arms, legs, hair, ears, or a hat. As the child begins to make
different kinds of images, she may take away some of the sun's rays or lengthen or short-
en others. In the figure on the far right, the radiating lines appear only on the top of the
head, where they could be interpreted as hair. Notice that the child used a curvy line on
the bottom of the face to show her daddy's beard.

For the adult, there may not seem to be much of a connection
between the way a scribble looks and what the child says about it. The
child may draw 4 lines and a circle and then say, "This is grandma's
garden. She's growing a tomato." But, regardless of what the adult
thinks of the scribble, it makes sense to the child. These allusions,
according to Howard Gardner in *Artful Scribbles*, not only allow the
child to speak about her drawing (and about the act of drawing itself)
but also to discuss what she initially wanted to accomplish. Even when
the child's intentions are not carried out (as when the child said she
was going to draw mommy but ended up with apples instead), she was
still describing what she originally wanted to draw.

The imaginative and often poetic comments that young children
make about their drawings may seem to come out of nowhere, but do

they really? Gardner refers to these allusions about prerepresentation-al drawings as *romancing*, a kind of fanciful commentary. He wonders whether the child really sees something in the drawing that no one else sees or whether the child is just trying to please adults who keep ask-ing her what the drawing is about. Another possibility, according to Gardner, is that romancing may be a way for the child to make the transition from pure scribbling to representational drawing.

But what about the child who is less verbal and doesn't (or can't) talk very much about her artwork? We should remember that visual art, like dance, instrumental music, and other kinds of creative expression, represents treasured forms of nonverbal communication. Sometimes colors, lines, and shapes say more than words ever could. Children should know that their paintings do not have to be *about* anything and do not *need* to be explained. They should get praise for their work whether they talk about it or not.

Space

In the early phases of scribbling, young children often scribble beyond the paper and draw over their old work. Later, they will stay within the margins of the paper and draw purposely around the marks they have previously made. Some scribblers notice (and respond to) the white or "empty" spaces on the page.

Color

Although young scribblers are more interested in making marks than they are in using colors, they should not be limited to only dark crayons and black felt-tip markers. Scribblers also enjoy painting, using play dough and other kinds of sensory materials. Because too many colors may distract the very young child, it is best to use colors sparingly.

The Preschematic Stage (4-7 Years Old)

The *Preschematic Stage* falls somewhere between the time that chil-dren go to nursery school and when they start formal education in kindergarten or first grade. This is an especially imaginative time for children, and one that is filled with unpredictable experiences for the adults who try to keep up with them. A trip to the pizza store to buy lunch can turn into an adventure as the child declares that he can't go out unless he puts on a special cape and carries his magic wand. Otherwise, he says, "The food won't come fast." Once on the street, he stops to look at a fire truck and then wonders if lizards like ice cream. In the restaurant, he hums a song out loud and then asks his dad why the bearded waiter has hairs on his chin and not his head.

The artwork of children this age is as exuberant and uninhibited as they are. It evolves out of scribbling activity that has been going on for years. Shortly after the child starts naming his scribbles, he begins producing drawings that are more controlled and more deliberate than they were before. The marks he makes are no longer associated only with body movement, but also with what the child wants to represent.

A child may start a painting with the intention of drawing a bicycle but the lines and shapes he makes may take him on a journey into the spontaneous representation of something else instead. Often, the first image we recognize is a figure, usually formed by a circle (i.e., mandala) for the head and body, and two lines coming out of it for the legs and feet. These kinds of *tadpole* representations come directly out of early mark-making that allowed the child to practice creating different

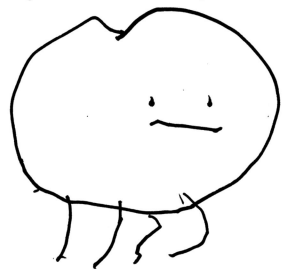

*Figure 5 - **Scribblers/Preschematics:*** Drawing by a 3½-year-old child. This 3½-year-old has formed a "tadpole" representation of a person. The bottom lines coming out of the circle suggest the evolution of this figure from the child's earlier drawings of the sun form. When this human image appeared on the page, the child looked a bit surprised. He said, "This is my friend. No, it's me at my house." Although the child is beginning to draw recognizable symbols and make verbal connections to them, he may still return to scribbling from time to time.

lines and shapes (see Figure 5). The child makes a cognitive connection between the shapes he is making and the shapes and objects that exist in the world. He begins to realize that the circle shape he has been drawing all this time is also the same shape as the sun, the center of a flower, the head or body of a person, or the shape of a beach ball. The square or rectangular shape he's been making could represent the bottom of a house. He might put a triangle on top of the square shape to represent the roof.

One of the most important aspects of the *Preschematic Stage* is that it is marked by the search for a *schema* (a way to represent objects). During this period, the child experiments with different ways of drawing. He is taking in stimuli at a very fast pace and drawing gives him a way to organize them into visual concepts. Each time he draws something, it will be different, depending on what he is thinking about at the time and what his most recent experiences have been. He may draw flowers looking like tulips one day and the next day he may draw them looking like daisies. If he just came back from the supermarket where he helped his mom carry heavy groceries, he is aware that it takes strong arms to lift things. The next time he draws someone carrying a package, the figure might have big arms because the child remembers how it felt to carry the groceries. If the figure carrying the bags is his mother, she may be depicted as bigger than everyone else in the picture because she feels big and powerful to him. Future drawings may show figures with small arms or no arms at all because arms may not be an important part of what the child is trying to express. Images for figures, houses, cars, dogs, etc., will keep on changing, until about the age of 7, when they stop becoming so variable and become more static.

Preschematic drawings tell us a lot about what is important to the child at this particular time in his life. These drawings have a fresh and spontaneous quality about them because they are created with total honesty and without forethought. The child is not worried about what things should look like or how to represent them true to form. He doesn't care about what is "right" or "wrong" or what is expected of him. His artwork may contain images of his family, friends, and pets or he may draw action figures, kings, queens, castles, dragons, imaginary bugs, or other kinds of fantasy creatures (see Figure 6). He draws whatever he wants to and he has fun with it. For him, artmaking is just another form of play. By the end of this period, he will have developed a vocabulary of flexible images that will vary, according to what is going on in his life at the time.

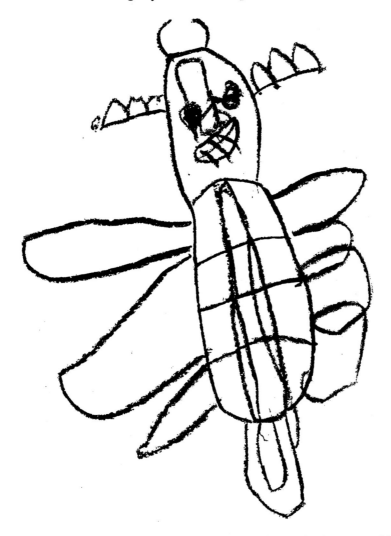

*Figure 6 - **Preschematics**:* Drawing by a 5-year-old child. This work of art exemplifies the active imagination of the young child and the uninhibited and playful way that he approaches drawing. As soon as he acquired some art materials, the child grabbed a crayon and started making elongated circular shapes. Letting one shape lead him to another, he came up with this fantasy creature, who has an insect body, a human-like face and long, pointed teeth. When asked about the picture, the child said, "It's an alien spider that can fly and swim. It can also bite."

Another important element to look at is the emotional and psychological role that drawing can provide for young children. We know that drawing is being used to explore the way the world works. One of the ways that children try to understand where they fit into the structure of things is through gender identification. In a society where the male and female messages in TV, toys, and the media strongly influence self-identity, children's artwork, even at a very young age, begins to pick up on gender stereotypes. Drawing provides the child with a safe place to try to figure out what it means to be a boy or a girl.

The child also uses art effectively to deal with powerful themes that reappear in adventure stories or action-oriented movies or TV shows. From the time that they first begin watching cartoons, children are exposed to fast-paced and often violent scenarios dealing with bad guys, scary monsters, and super-heroes. The child is using the medium of art, not only to deal with his own internal fears, thoughts, and feelings, but also to sort out dichotomies like good and evil, and power and weakness. Art provides a structure for conceptual organization. Said another way, art helps him think (see Figure 7).

*Figure 7 - **Preschematics:*** Drawing by a 6-year-old child. In dramatic play and in artwork, this child spent a lot of time exploring themes connected to "strength" and "weakness." This drawing shows the child trying to create "Robot Man," the strongest man in the world (even stronger than Batman). On the left is Batman and on the right is Robot Man. The child is trying to figure out what characteristics Robot Man would need in order to be stronger than all of the bad forces in the world. To make him really strong, the child said that he would have to be made out of steel. He showed him as having a rigid-looking body and a mean look on his face. (Batman looks much sweeter.) The child differentiated Robot Man from Batman by putting a different insignia on his shirt and some special contraptions on his belt.

Space

Spatial relationships appear as they feel to the child and not as they look to adults. In a young child's egocentric universe, objects revolve around him, and space is a container to hold things in place. When the child thinks of himself in the world, he is not thinking in a linear or literal way. Although he may perceive the sky above and the ground below, he doesn't see himself standing on a flat surface next to something planted in the earth like a tree. Rather, he thinks of objects as they connect to his life, not as they neatly line up on a picture plane. Drawings usually depict objects floating around the page in a way that makes sense to the child (see Figures 8 & 9).

*Figure 8 - **Preschematics**:* Drawing by a 6½-year-old child. While this child is aware of the sky above (notice the skyline) and the ground below (notice the bumpy baseline), she doesn't think of herself as logically standing on a flat surface. She draws things as she experiences or imagines them. The flowers are portrayed as lollipop circles with V-shaped leaves and the sun is made of rainbows. The child and the bunny (who may be jumping) look happy and carefree as they are magically elevated above the ground.

*Figure 9 - **Preschematics**:* Drawing by a 6½-year-old child. This drawing was made just weeks after Figure 8 (done by the same child). The skyline is gone and the baseline is flat. The sun is a solid mass with rays coming out of it and the lollipop flowers have no leaves. The girl and the imaginary animals are happily floating in the air, far away from the ground. The child is showing us how she thinks about the world and how it feels to her. Her sense of space is very subjective. She thinks of objects as they revolve around her, not as they look to others. During this developmental stage, each time the child draws something, it will look different, depending on her experiences and what is going on in her life at the time.

Color

Color is used for its own sake and not to illustrate an objective universe. There may be no relationship between the color chosen to paint an object and the actual color of the object being represented. People may be red, green, yellow, or purple and houses may be painted in bold stripes, blue dots, or silver squares. The child is not consciously using color for emotive purposes (as are adult expressionist artists) but just because he has not yet taken in the adult version of how things are supposed to look. If adults try to manipulate this stage by telling the child that he should use *realistic* colors, the child will probably do what he is told. Like most of us, he likes praise. But the child needs to make his own choices. He is not developmentally ready to deal with the adult version of reality, and it would be inappropriate, at best, to try to change his original vision.

The Schematic Stage (7-9 Years Old)

The child of this age may be involved with activities such as team sports, learning to play an instrument, reading books, and riding a bike. Gaining a little more independence, she might be going to a friend's house by herself, walking around the neighborhood or coming home from school alone. Relationships have broadened and friendships have taken on more meaning. Now the child cares more about what people say, what they feel, and what they think about things. She is better able to share with others and take in different points of view.

Because children are less egocentric than they were before, they now draw themselves as a part of the environment rather than as the center of it. When they draw buildings, a tree, or a bicycle, they draw themselves in relationship to those things and in proportion to them. Whereas in the past, the child may have depicted herself larger than a house, now the house is larger than she is.

At about this time in the child's artistic development, her artwork reflects the use of a *schema* (a generic symbol for objects). The schema usually consists of simple, geometric forms that represent the child's active knowledge of a subject. Once the child has formed a concept for a person, a tree, or a house, she will apply it again and again. The schema becomes a formula and a safety net that the child reaches for whenever she needs to express something. When there are no important new experiences that the child has had with a particular subject, the schema stays the same. However, if something dramatic happens, the child may go beyond the symbols ordinarily used.

For example, a dog may be depicted the same way repeatedly until one day the child gets a new puppy. At that point, the schema may be modified and expanded because the experience of having the puppy has stimulated the child to make a more personal and expressive statement. Before she got her puppy, the child's drawing of a dog may have consisted of a circle for a head, two ears, and a long body with four legs and a tail. After the child is given the puppy, the drawing may keep the same general structure, but it might be larger and

contain more detail than the previous drawings. The child will probably pay more attention to certain areas of the dog's anatomy, like the
ears. The puppy's face may even have a human expression. The
texture or spots on the puppy's fur may also be highlighted. The closer the child feels to the dog, the more the drawing will look like the
child's puppy and not just a generic dog. Generally, if the child has
had a strong bonding experience with something (in this case, the
puppy), that experience will show up in imagery that not only illus-
trates knowledge of the subject, but also has emotional meaning for
the child.

Also, if a child is involved with certain kinds of imaginary play characters such as super-heroes, dolls, comic strip characters, prehistoric
animals (like dinosaurs), or mythological creatures (like centaurs), her
schema for them may develop and become very flexible and personal. She may go way beyond the usual smiling face and similar body
type when painting these characters because they mean so much to
her. She has learned a great deal about them and her drawings reflect
that knowledge. Each time she draws one of these important characters, the facial expressions, the movement of the figures, as well as
other distinguishing details may be different (see Figure 10).

*Figure 10 - **Schematics***: Drawing by a 7-year-old child. This child developed rich and flexible schemas for a large range of "good" and "bad" fantasy characters that he played with and watched on television and in the movies. Although the characters he created were often similar versions of established super-heroes like Batman and Robin, he was still able to make them his own by changing their facial expressions and their costumes. He also liked to make up new and intricate scenarios for them to act out. This drawing shows one of the characters using a sword and another one brandishing a magic ball. One of the bad guys (the Joker) is carrying a cane that has special, destructive powers. This kind of drawing is an example of a child using art to help him sort through big themes like good and evil and power and weakness.

Family portraits and other figurative drawings provide clues that reveal how the child perceives the world at this age. These drawings show us how much the child knows about the human body and how she sees herself in relationship to other people. Human figures are often depicted face-forward, in a bold and flat manner. Sometimes all of the family members will have the same faces and the same geometrically structured body shapes. To differentiate men from women, and boys from girls, the child may dress the figures differently (in pants, dresses, high heels or baseball caps). Most often adults are depicted as larger than the children. The images produced eventually merge into *fixed* schematic representations that get repeated for a period of time (see Figure 11). The child will change the images when something important happens to her or when she is emotionally and developmentally ready to let them go.

Figure 11 - Schematics: Painting by an 8-year-old child. Asked to draw a pretend family, this child drew two parents and a lot of siblings. The mother is at the center of the picture and the father is on the right. The child's schema for all of the figures stays fixed, possibly because the characters are imaginary and they do not have any particular emotional meaning for her. If she created a portrait of her real family, she might have shown more individualized physical characteristics such as her sister's new hair style, her mom's trademark hat and sunglasses, and her dad's bushy beard. Notice that the child is beginning to develop a concept of depth by putting the little boy in front of his dad and the little girl in front of her mom.

Regardless of what children this age draw, they are often concerned with some aspect of getting things "right." In reflecting upon this concern, we may think that the onset of elementary school, with its ever-present preoccupation with rules and conventions, explains the child's shift toward correctness. (The child may come home from school and announce that she has just learned the *exact* way to draw a tree.) However, normal developmental changes and social pressures play heavily on the child's attitudes and interests, whether she attends a traditional school setting or not. For the child, the creation of a schema is an important way for her to use symbolic language in order to establish a format for self-expression. The child feels secure whenever she reaches into her arsenal of schematic images in order to explore a theme or express an idea. As long as the child is able to change the schema when an important event or experience occurs, she is still using images creatively.

But there can be a problem when the child persists in using a rigid schema that shows no personal or emotional involvement with the subject. For instance, stereotypic images like rainbows and a smiling sun with radiating lines coming out of it may be used by the child whenever anyone asks her to draw something. Also, some children this age create and repeat schemas that are more influenced by cartoon and comic book characters than they are by the child's own experience. These pictures give the impression that the child does not have enough confidence in herself to draw the world the way she sees it and knows it best. Sometimes these drawings can be so small and tentative that it feels as if the child is not sure that they actually deserve a place on the page. (See Chapter 4, under *Schematics*, for ways to work with stereotypic images.)

During the *Schematic Stage*, the child is synthesizing a lot of information at school, at home, and in a world that is getting bigger all the time. Her artwork reflects a struggle to understand concepts that keep changing. This is a time when many children may lose confidence in their artistic abilities. If art expression, in any form that makes sense to the child, is not supported and valued in the home and school, many children may stop drawing altogether.

Space

The big change at this stage is that the child is now aware that there is order in spatial relationships. To clarify that objects and people don't really float in space, the child often establishes a baseline (and sometimes a skyline) on almost all of her pictures. The baseline is essentially a line (or lines) at the bottom of the page on which people and other important objects stand. The skyline is a line at the top of the page that implies that the sky ends at a certain point. Between the ground and the sky there is an empty area symbolizing air. The appearance of the baseline represents the child's acute awareness that she is an interactive part of the environment.

Sometimes the baseline schema will vary or may even disappear altogether, depending on the experience the child intends to portray. There are some very interesting and creative ways that children represent space at this age. The following are examples:

Aerial View–Drawing something from a high angle, as if you are looking down at it from an airplane.
X-ray Vision–Showing the inside and the outside of something at the same time (see Figure 12).

*Figure 12 - **Schematics***: Painting by a 7-year-old child. In this painting, the child, using *x-ray vision*, is showing us how much she knows about her house. We can see it from the inside (as with the closet on the second level) and the outside (as with the garage door on the bottom left) at the same time. On the bottom right, the child is standing by the front door. It looks like she just found a shoe. Stairs are shown, leading up to all the floors, giving us a very good idea of the general layout of her house. Her mom is on the second floor, standing in front of a doorway and her little brother is playing upstairs.

Folding Over–Objects appear to be upside down, such as the way images look when they are reflected in the water (see Figure 13).

Space and Time Representations–Synthesizing various time sequences into one drawing (comic strips are good examples of this).

Plan and Elevation Drawings–Drawings that show objects from several different views at the same time, such as tables tipped forward or dishes turned toward the viewer instead of lying flat on the table.

Figure 13 - Schematics: Painting by a 7-year-old child. This painting shows the child standing in front of her house. After she drew herself on the sidewalk, she turned the paper around so that she could draw the house across the street. We see the house as being upside down (or *folded over*), but the child doesn't think of it that way. She is simply showing us a subjective view of what both sides of the street look like.

Color

An exciting artistic discovery for the child at this age is that there is a relationship between an object and a specific color. Whereas during the *Preschematic Stage* (4-7), the child chooses colors randomly (sometimes unconsciously achieving strong emotional effect), she is now interested in getting the colors "right." Grass gets painted green, the sky is a perfect shade of blue, and the sun is solid yellow. Just as the schema for the human figure and other objects stays the same, the relationships of colors to objects will also remain constant. Once the child has begun painting the sky blue, it will stay that way unless a direct experience temporarily changes the schema. For example, a child playing outdoors notices that before a thunderstorm the sky turns an ominous, dark color. After an experience like that, her view of the sky may change and her use of color may become more expansive.

The child wants to control color and may not be comfortable when paint runs together during the painting process. These spontaneous and accidental happenings, so much a part of the art experience, may now be looked upon by the child as "mistakes."

The Dawning Realist Stage (9-12 Years Old)

The older child may still be playing sports, taking music lessons, and riding bikes, but something is different. He is losing the sense of safety and innocence that defines childhood. The discovery that his parents don't have all the answers makes the world feel like a bigger and scarier place. At this stage in life, the older child is beginning to explore things a little more and he is starting to define his own space. He has his own ideas about things and he doesn't always believe what adults tell him. In fact, he has begun to question authority. One of the ways that he can establish himself as more of his own person is through identifying and bonding with peers.

Group activities and spending time with friends fills a crucial need. At times, the dynamics of the group become more important to him than his own emotional needs and desires. This may not be an easy time for the older child because as his social life expands, he may also be getting more self-conscious about how he looks and how he is perceived by others. Often, family members think of him as being petulant and moody. His emotional life may become more private as he shares more intimacies with his friends than with family.

After the age of 9 or so, most children's drawings reflect a change from their earlier schema. The new drawings usually show an awareness of sexual characteristics and changing body image. But, if the schema remains sexually neutral, it is probably because the older child is not yet ready to deal with physical maturation and the looming issue of sexuality. Drawings during this period may be a bit stiff, awkward, and formal. Details, designs, and decorative features may become important elements of artwork because children this age tend to be interested in even the most minute aspects of visual appearance.

When drawing a person, the older child may include the pattern of someone's shirt, the buttons on the coat, a belt, the person's eyelashes, shoelaces on the sneakers, and even blemishes or beauty marks on the skin. Instead of using distortion, exaggeration, and expressionistic color as he did when he was younger, the older child will now substitute details for things that have particular emotional significance for him. In doodles or sketches, he may also invent prototype characters that he uses repeatedly in his work. These kinds of characters can sometimes take on a life of their own as the older child becomes involved with making up adventurous scenarios for them and changing their clothes and hairstyles (see Figure 14).

*Figure 14 - **Dawning Realists:** Drawing by an 11-year-old child. This student created a character that was used often to explore and observe body language and clothing styles. In this drawing, there are 7 versions of him. Some of the figures have their arms by their sides and some of them are moving their hands in different directions. In each of the drawings, something about the character changes, like hairstyle, facial hair, short or long pants, solid, light, dark, or checkered shirts. The student pays close attention to clothing details, like length of pants, short or long sleeve shirts, and even string-ties on a sweatshirt.*

If art has not been a consistent part of their lives, some older children may bring a certain amount of anxiety and self-consciousness to the experience. The more insecure the student is, the more he may think about "getting it right." For some students, "getting it right" might mean copying something *exactly* from a magazine, a comic book, or a friend's sketchbook. At this age, copying may provide a way for the older child to hold on to something real and instantly successful. Developmentally, the older child is approaching a place where he is acquiring skills that will allow him to leave the schema behind. But he is not sure that he is good enough to draw what he wants. Neatness, accuracy, even some idea of perfection (whatever that is) can become the unattainable goal. Because a lot of older children don't want to make "mistakes," some of them may prefer to use sharpened pencils with erasers rather than art materials that are harder to control, such as paint. Often, as the older child works, he can be seen erasing his drawing, looking disappointed, and claiming that he has "messed up."

Drawings at this age are not usually involved with representing the world accurately, but about characterizing it. In other words, the artwork is about how older children think the world is supposed to look, and how the culture influences what they see. Idealized pop culture icons such as sports figures, body builders, comic book heroes, supermodels, movie and music stars all play heavily into images that children create during this period (see Figures 15, 16, & 17). Both boys and girls begin to pay more attention to their bodies and they start thinking about their imperfections. Drawings often reflect exaggerated gender stereotypes of what boys and girls think they should look like.

*Figure 15 - **Dawning Realists**:* Drawing by an 11-year-old child. This student used baseball cards and other kinds of pictures as references for drawings of sports figures and other action figures. This work shows an effort to represent the body in proportion and also to show the movement of the baseball player just before he hit the ball.

*Figure 16 - **Dawning Realists**:* Drawing by a 12-year-old child. This sketch of a football player shows an attempt to draw correct body proportions. The student has paid close attention to the football player's uniform. Notice the helmet, belt, leg and shoulder pads, and drawstring pants.

*Figure 17 - **Dawning Realists:** Drawing by a 10-year-old child. Many students this age are beginning to be interested in physical appearance and the structure of the human body. This student drew two versions of a He-Man body builder. Notice the x-ray view of the muscles. The student portrays them as U shapes inside the big strong arms and as square shapes inside the chest and stomach.

Artistically, the student is in a holding pattern. He has lost his uninhibited and free-form approach to artmaking. With the safe and comfortable schema no longer age-appropriate, the older child is in a place where there are no easy answers. Making art still meets a strong internal need, but the student feels insecure about how to proceed. He knows that there is no clear-cut way to create a work of art, and there are few people to ask for guidance. The older child is also very sensitive about being judged. He wants to express himself, but still, he is not sure if he is "good" enough or what people will think of his work.

Space

The older child is aware that the baseline and skyline format previously used to define the borders of the universe is not just an oversimplification, it is also inaccurate. He knows that the sky is infinite and endless, the ground is not really flat, and objects in space can be in front or in back of one another.

As the baseline begins to disappear, objects cease to stand on an artificially constructed edge. The old baseline moves up from the bottom of the page to the lower half or even the center of the page. It now takes the form of a horizon line which gives the child a starting point for eventually exploring techniques which will create the illusion of depth and perspective.

Color

As the preteen matures, he sees colors more as a characterization than a definitive "truth." The preadolescent perceives color more in gradations of tone than in the bold, flat colors of the *Schematic Stage*. He now describes the color of a car as being bluish-green, rather than solid blue.

The Pseudo-Naturalist Stage (12-14 Years Old)

This stage marks the formal beginning of young adolescence. According to the Swiss psychologist Jean Piaget, the young teenager has entered a period of mental development where she is now capable of abstract thought and deductive reasoning. When the teen was younger, she was primarily focused on the present moment. Now she thinks about the future and she can also deal with hypothetical situations. She can look at a problem from several points of view and figure out how to solve it. During this stage and beyond, the teenager is also developing her own inner value system and a sense of moral judgment.

As she begins to question everything around her, the young teen may be thrown into a turbulent period marked by rebelliousness, anger, alienation, depression, and self-criticism. During this insecure time, she continues loosening ties with family and forms even tighter bonds with peers. She cares a lot about how she looks and what other people think of her. The fact that she is developing sexual characteristics and becoming taller or staying shorter than she might want to be, may make her feel out of control. But, even though at times she may look like an adult (and sometimes she tries to act like one), she may still have the emotional make-up of a child.

Young adolescents categorize each other according to criteria such as who they spend time with, what they wear, how they style their hair, whether or not they excel in sports, if they are fat or thin, tall or short, what kind of music they listen to, and if they are well-liked. No matter where the young adolescent fits into the peer group social strata, this is bound to be a time of insecurity and confusion. For many teens, the struggle to be popular, to be considered cool, and to fit in never ends.

Artistically, young adolescents continue to be self-conscious and less spontaneous about their artwork than they used to be. Rather than take out some art materials and just play around with them, they are more likely to carefully plan out their drawings. Some teens are especially interested in drawing from nature (i.e., still life objects, the figure, or landscapes), while other teens like to create fantasy drawings. Since the young adolescent is attuned to what other people are doing and saying around her, she is also critically aware of her own art. She is very product-oriented and really strives for success. In art projects, that means that the final piece has to come out "right." She shows great frustration and disdain for her work when it doesn't look the way she wants it to.

Not only is artmaking less spontaneous for teens, but it also can be more sporadic than it was before. The young teen may need more support and stimulation from caring adults in order to continue working. Some themes that help to draw adolescents back into making art are portraits of rock stars and other pop culture heroes (see Figure 18), as well as imaginary and exaggerated characters (see Figure 19).

*Figure 18 - **Pseudo-Naturalists:*** Print by a 14-year-old teen. The teenager who made this linoleum print was very involved with music, even playing in a number of student jazz and rock bands. Part of what makes this portrait of a pop singer interesting is the way it is composed. The image is simple and direct, and the overall effect is bold and dynamic. The student did not distract us with complicated or irrelevant details. He showed us only the reggae singer, the microphone, the speaker, and the word "Rasta" on the wall.

*Figure 19 - **Pseudo-Naturalists:*** Drawing by a 13-year-old teen. Astute observational skills and a good sense of humor were effectively used to characterize a large range of human facial expressions. At first, the 3 men look like 3 different characters. But on closer examination, they may also be variations of the same person. The facial features are the same, but the shape of the head, the movement of the mouth, the wrinkles on the forehead, the lines under the eyes, and the hairstyles are all different. Some of the expressions in the drawing could be interpreted as surprise, seriousness, and silliness. Note the exaggeration of the jowls.

Thankfully, doodling provides young teens with an easy and non-threatening way to stay involved with art. Often, school notebooks, scraps of paper, and old napkins reveal interesting drawings of sports figures, cartoons, designs with lettering or patterns, and overly sexualized, satirical, funny, or grotesque characters. Just as many of us didn't think much about the young child's scribbles, we may also pay little attention to these adolescent doodles. But, for some teens, they are the main form of art produced during this period. They can be surprisingly sophisticated and fascinating to look at, sometimes revealing subconscious thoughts and fantasies. Because doodles are considered throw-away art or scrap, the young adolescent may feel less inhibited about expressing herself in this art form. With doodles, she doesn't worry as much about being evaluated. Doodling is also a good way for teens to work out creative ideas, develop original characters, and find new ways to use art materials (see Figures 20 & 21).

*Figure 20 - **Pseudo-Naturalists:*** Drawing by a 14-year-old teen. This doodle drawing gives us a glimpse into what the student is daydreaming about. He has created some inventive and exaggerated characters that are fun to look at. To make them stand out from one another, the student changed the shape of the faces, the hair, facial expressions, and hats. Some of these characters look confused, angry, mean, funny, or goofy. In addition to these oddball characters, fish are also floating around the page.

*Figure 21 - **Pseudo-Naturalists**:* Drawing by a 13-year-old teen. When she was about 12 years old, this student created what she calls a "Skippy" cartoon character. Skippy is a prototype person (a universal every person) who has no color, no gender, and no age. In this drawing Skippy walks, jumps, dances, stands still, sits down, puts one hand up, one hand down, lies down, and does back flips.

Because adolescence is a traditional time for teens to experiment, some of them may get involved with adventurous physical and social activities. Their artwork often expresses this new sense of "being on the edge" and courting danger. If the young adolescent's drawings are involved with violent and/or sexual themes, artwork at this age can carry with it a stigma of shame and embarrassment. The young teen may still want to hide her drawings from teachers, family, and friends because of her insecurity about it. She may not know what kind of feedback she will get from people, and she doesn't want to deal with disapproval. If adults or peers say something demeaning or insensitive about her artwork, the student may be even more reticent about continuing.

Space

As the young teenager begins noticing the size reduction of distant objects, she may become interested in representing perspective and three-dimensional space. For some students, these kinds of skills become exciting new tools for art expression. For others, they are irrelevant additions to their visual vocabulary.

Color

Young adolescents have a heightened sense of color, fashion, and style. Many teens are buying their own clothes and putting together inventive and dynamic outfits. As they start exploring their individuality, their involvement with color intensifies. The way they dress and the colors they wear become important aspects of how they want to be seen and known by other people, especially their peers. In their artwork, color may reflect objective reality or it may be used primarily for emotional effect. Although students can be taught about the formal properties of color, sometimes through the use of color wheels, this kind of teaching may inhibit their free expression. The most important aspect of color is the student's intuitive reaction to it and how she chooses to use it.

Adolescent Art (14-17 Years Old)

For many people, full-blown adolescence is the most anxiety-ridden stage in the human life cycle. It is not hard to see why. During the time that the young person is developing the biological characteristics of adulthood, he is supposed to grow up and finally leave childhood behind. But he cannot grow up until he separates from the people he's been closest to and begins the process of searching for an independent sense of self. This transition can be monumental for some teens, but in this culture, we normalize the change and deny its emotional impact on the child. Compared to the attention and affection that society (at least superficially) showers on the young child, the adolescent is either ignored or thought of as an annoyance or, in some cases, a threat. Many teens alienate the very people whom they depend on for support in their attempt to separate from parents and other adults in positions of authority. Sometimes, a part of the struggle to individuate involves pushing people away. As a society, we do not acknowledge or deal with the anger, loss, separation, and confusion that teenagers experience during this stage. Still, we expect an independent and responsible adult to emerge out of a time of turmoil. In *Identity: Youth and Crisis*, Erik Erikson says, "The final assembly of all the converging identity elements at the end of childhood (and the abandonment of the divergent ones) appears to be a formidable task: how can a stage as 'abnormal' as adolescence be trusted to accomplish it?" [5]

In order to begin this formidable search for self, most teenagers have to become critical of themselves, their parents, teachers, authority figures, and society in general. They question everything, including their artistic creations. In earlier stages of artistic development, older children created drawings that reflected the way they thought things were supposed to look. Later, young adolescents tried to draw the human body as well as other images in nature. During this final stage of adolescence, students start to become interested in how they can see and think for themselves. Their work becomes more thoughtful and self-reflective.

Instead of asking, "How are things supposed to look?" or "How can I draw from nature?" they start wondering, "What do I really see?" and "How do I feel about it?" Pop culture also plays an enormous role in how teenagers think about things, how they view themselves, and what they think is important. They are very caught up with physical appearance and standards of beauty set out by the culture. Although these standards are not possible for most people to meet, they still affect teenage self-esteem. Often, the self-portraits and doodles of adolescent students reveal a distorted body image and a preoccupation with what they perceive to be their own physical flaws. Student artwork around this time also reflects a developing sexuality (and that includes sexual orientation). Drawings may show wide interpretations of male and female characteristics.

---

5. Erik H. Erikson, *Identity: Youth and Crisis.* New York: W.W. Norton and Company, 1994, p.163.

At this age, students have begun to make their own decisions about what kind of work they want to do and how they want to do it. Because cultural, social, and historical influences are so important, adolescent art often takes on a derivative form. Teens may become attracted to a certain artist, historical movement, or style of painting and then work in that style for a period of time. This can be seen as a creative exploration for the student if he allows it to expand his growth (see Figure 22). But appropriation of another artist's style may not be beneficial if a student gets stuck repeating the same image over and over.

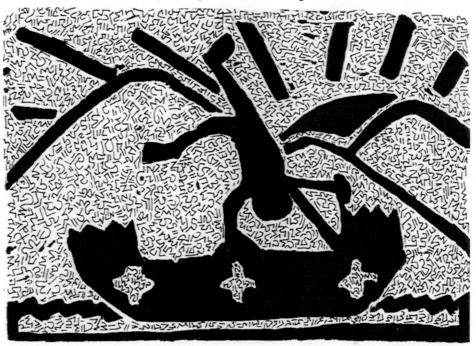

*Figure 22 - **Adolescent Art:*** Drawing by 14-year-old teen. The work of graffiti-inspired artist Keith Haring was introduced to this student about 3 years before she did this ink drawing. When she first saw his art she was very excited about it and has been influenced by him ever since. Ironically, she was creating characters that looked a little bit like the ones he was painting, even before she ever heard of him. In this drawing, the simple, expressive shapes, the energy of the figure, and the intricate design elements in the background are all reminiscent of Haring's style. But while the student has integrated some of his concepts into her art, she has held on to original ideas and continued expanding and developing her own work.

This is a time for students to take in many influences and experiment with a variety of styles. Some students work primarily from life or from their imagination, while others would rather get ideas from pre-existing visual material, such as comic strips, fashion magazines, or art books. Naturalism can be a popular mode of expression for teens as they become interested in the realistic depiction of shadows, folds, wrinkles, textures in common objects, and depth and perspective. Portraits of people often show a serious attempt at modelling (see Figures 23 & 24).

*Figure 23 - **Adolescent Art**:* Drawing by a 15-year-old teen. Pop stars tend to be a favorite subject for teenagers to draw. In this rendition of a British rock star (done from a photograph), the student took a naturalistic approach to the subject. Shadows around the face and under the chin are highlighted, as well as other details of interest like the faint stubble of a beard, earrings, and a necklace.

*Figure 24 - **Adolescent Art***: Drawing by a 17-year-old teen. This student created a very sensitive and well-crafted portrait through careful observation of form and attention to modelling. The drawing has a realistic feeling about it and, not surprisingly, was done from a live model. The student established a three-dimensional sculptural quality by using white crayon on the lighter areas and dark pencil to form the shadows.

Cartoon images are another form of art that interests teens. They can be used playfully to make fun of authority figures that have a prominent role in their lives and to satirize the culture. Some students at this age work expressionistically, using color and distorted form to establish symbolic and emotional meaning (see Figure 25). Occasionally, teens also work with pure abstraction.

*Figure 25 - **Adolescent Art**:* Print by a 14-year old-teen. This powerful and scary creature was made by cutting into a linoleum block with a sharp tool. It is unclear if the creature is human or animal, real, or imaginary. The expressionistic scream could be coming from a place of power or fear, or it could be a metaphorical image representing any other state of mind or emotion. Before doing this print, the student had been very interested in looking at African masks.

A style of art that has become especially popular among teenagers in recent years is graffiti. Because graffiti is illegal, street artists (also called *taggers* or *writers*) sign their work with made-up names or initials. These anonymous names, letters, or words establish a new identity for the teen and often become the artistic focus of the work (see Figure 52 in Chapter 6 for an example). While most adults think of graffiti as vandalism, it has been embraced as an art form by an international youth culture, the music scene (especially hip-hop), and the established art world. Originally found on the walls of the city of Pompeii, Italy, in the first century AD, graffiti has been around for a long time. It has always been a controversial and underground voice of alienation and rebellion. In recent years, graffiti art (art in the style of graffiti but created on paper or canvas instead of on buildings or subway cars) has become a popular vehicle of self-expression for middle-class, suburban youth as well as for teens from the inner city.

Regardless of whether teens are creating graffiti because they want to mark territory, get recognition from peers, establish that they exist, or because they are angry at society, they are still acting out an undeniable impulse to make art. In fact, graffiti has been a source of creative thinking and innovation for many teens, even keeping some of them out of gangs. Experienced graffiti writers consider themselves to be serious calligraphers as well as innovators of a secret language, like hieroglyphics. According to Michael Walsh, author of *Graffito,* graffiti writers want us to see their work, but they don't necessarily want us to understand it.

Whether teens are taking formal art classes at school, doodling on a ripped paper napkin, painting a mural on the side of a building, or creating graffiti, they are using art to discover something new about themselves and the world. Making art is a way for them to push limits in a constructive and introspective way. Because artmaking is essentially a dialogue with the self, it can represent one of the few places where teens feel safe enough to project ideas, feelings, fantasies, and fears.

Space

Teenagers expand their interpretation of space by reaching a point in their artistic development where they are able to take in the world in a more naturalistic and less idealized way. Drawings may begin to show the illusion of perspective and depth as some students become very skilled at portraying three-dimensional space on paper. An example of this can be seen in sophisticated forms of graffiti, where letters and words look practically sculptural. Other students may explore a flatter, more expressionistic interpretation of space, sometimes achieving an emotional and psychological effect.

Color

Color is now used in a very individualistic way, just as it would be with adults. For students who take on a more literal approach to art-making, color is depicted as close as possible to its surface appearance. For those who work more abstractly, color may be used for aesthetic or expressionistic purposes rather than as a way to define objective reality.

The next chapter provides ideas to help parents and teachers nurture children and adolescents throughout all of the stages of artistic development.

Chapter 4
KEEPING CREATIVITY ALIVE

SUPPORTING CHILDREN FROM SCRIBBLERS TO
ADOLESCENT ARTISTS

Although children are naturally creative, at some point in time (usually after the age of 7 or so), many of them begin to lose confidence in their own artwork. Children may say, "I'm not good at art," and they really believe it. Often they become so discouraged with what they perceive as their inability to draw, that many children completely stop making art. By the time they enter adulthood, it can be difficult for them to recover their innate artistic abilities. To prevent this from happening during any of the stages of development, we need to look at ways that we, as parents and teachers, can help our children emerge from social, educational, and cultural influences with their creativity still intact.

We know that children need adults in their lives who are caring, consistent, and supportive. But they also need access to adults who are connected to the creative spirit and who want to nurture it. When overseeing art projects with children, we should have an open mind and an attitude that encourages curiosity. Because children are so influenced by adult aesthetic judgment and standards of beauty, their unique vision can easily get compromised. No two people see the world the same way, yet the impressionable child will often mimic the adult version of what looks "right." When this happens, the child draws inauthentic and stereotyped images that reflect what she thinks other people want to look at, not what she really sees or imagines. As parents and teachers, we should encourage our children to use art as a vehicle for creative exploration and self-expression, not as a tool to please other people.

64

One way to encourage our children's artistic efforts is first to give them support for the work they are doing and then ask questions that can stimulate the child to take the work even further. For instance, if a young child shows an adult a drawing of a figure on a big, blank page, the adult might say, "Tell me more about this person. Who is she? Where does she live? How old is she? Is she going for a walk? Is it cold outside?" The questions may elicit an elaborate visual scenario for the child that may not have existed before.

Working through art projects not only gives children experience in creative problem-solving, it also lets them see firsthand what it is like to deal with uncertainty and frustration. Because there is no right or wrong way to make art, and because there are no fixed answers, some children may feel a bit unsure about their work. Some of the insecurity they feel is tied up with how other people react to it. The elementary school child begins to wonder, "Is this OK? Am I a good artist? Is the teacher going to like this? Will the other kids like it? What will my mom and dad think?" If the child is so focused on getting approval, she may miss out on a lot of the fun and experimentation that is so much a part of creating art.

Our educational system contributes to this creative disconnection when it fosters art programs that disregard the integrity of the imaginative child. We have all seen holiday projects that utilize stereotypic images of Christmas trees, Halloween pumpkins, or Thanksgiving turkeys. These projects make children think that there is a *correct* way to draw or paint things. As the child is working, she is more likely to be wondering, "Did I get it right?" than she is to be thinking, "What color do I feel like using?" Often, the child who goes home with an image that looks different from everyone else's feels that she did something wrong. Children are not being creatively challenged when they are coloring by number or within designated shapes, trying to copy someone else's picture, or completing prefabricated art assignments that have limited and predicable results.

It is important to note that school is not the only source of the problem. There are also ways that we interact with our children and adolescents that have negative and sometimes smothering effects. Teresa Amabile, author of *Creativity in Context*, identifies 7 main "Creativity Killers." They are:

1. Surveillance—We all need space in order to create. No one likes to have someone leaning over her shoulder while she is working on something important. Children and adolescents are no exception.

2. Evaluation—It is very difficult to create original work while worrying about what someone else thinks of it. We should support our children's creative efforts and not make them feel that they are being judged. The act of judging art is itself a bit tricky, since it is a highly subjective enterprise. Artmaking is a process of learning that keeps changing over time. Through their art, children are telling us about their experience. They are speaking in images, not words. Instead of deciding what is good and bad, we need to pay attention to what they are saying.

3. Rewards—For many artists, rewards (although sometimes necessary to continue the work) add an emotional and psychological burden to the already delicate and unpredictable act of creating. In *The Social Psychology of Creativity*, Amabile says, "It appears that when people are primarily motivated to do some creative activity by their own interest in and enjoyment of that activity, they may be more creative than they are when primarily motivated by some goal imposed on them by others."[6] Amabile studied the negative effects of prizes, public recognition, book contracts, and other rewards on the lives of famous writers such as Sylvia Plath, Thomas Wolfe, Anne Sexton, and T.S. Eliot. All of them had great difficulty dealing with success, which is supposed to be the ultimate reward. After receiving a Nobel Prize in literature, T.S. Eliot referred to it as "a ticket to one's own funeral."[7]

For children, motivation such as toys, candy, or a trip to the zoo can only go so far. When we see our children spend intense time engaged in dramatic play, making music, solving puzzles, building things, or writing stories, it is because they choose to and not because of an extrinsic reward. The motivation for sustained creative work comes from a deep internal source, whether it is intellectual, emotional, or psychological. The best reward is the one that celebrates the intuitive part of ourselves that creates because we need to, or want to, not because we are looking for approval, or seeking a prize.

4. Competition—Competition is based on the premise that someone is more skilled than someone else. That works well in sports

---

6. Teresa M. Amabile, *The Social Psychology of Creativity.* New York: Springer-Verlag, 1983, p.15.
7. Ibid., p.13.

because there is objective evidence to prove who was stronger, faster, or more agile. In art, competitions make little sense because they utilize subjective criteria. We are not dealing with who can run the fastest mile, but who is thought by whom to be a better artist. If the judges have a preference for realistic-looking work, and the child/adolescent expresses herself in big, abstract shapes, she is probably not going to win. Furthermore, competitions force people to ask, "What do the judges like?" That in itself is damaging to the creative spirit.

5. Overcontrol—We are constantly telling our young children and teenagers what to do and how to do it. When they are young, we tell them who to play with, how to dress, and what to eat for lunch. When they reach adolescence, we tell them what classes to take, what time to be home, the "right" way to fix their room, and the "best" way to study.

The problem with this is that what works for one person does not always work for another. We need to give our children and adolescents the space they need to experiment with finding ways to do things that work for them, not us, while at the same time securing their safety.

6. Restricting choices—Channeling children into activities that parents approve of can backfire when children aren't allowed to try out things that they might find fulfilling. I believe that we should allow children to follow their creative passions. If exposed to a variety of stimuli, children will choose the subject that intrigues them the most. Our job, as parents and teachers, is to support that interest.

In the arts, we need to be careful not to push our children into one style over another. In the visual arts, realism is not *better* than abstraction, just as in music, classical is not *better* than jazz. If parents and teachers push one style over another, the child may begin to feel that the only way to get approval is to create the kind of work that adults like.

7. Pressure—Creative activity comes out of enjoyment, not pressure. Parents and teachers who push too hard will often turn children off.

Pushing too hard can mean imposing unrealistic expectations on our children, overscheduling them, or making every activity into a performance. A child who is intrinsically motivated to do something, like play the piano, is practicing because she needs to explore something, not because an authority figure demanded that she play.

Working with Scribblers (2 or Younger–4 Years Old)

For the young child, scribbling is very important work. It represents a universal primary process that children go through as they search for language, expand their motor abilities, and try to figure out what their connection is to the rest of the world. While scribbles may look to us like nothing more than random lines on a page, they really offer a wellspring of information about the child's cognitive growth. Over a period of time, these drawings give us a lot of insight into how the child is thinking, changing, and developing.

Since the young scribbler works in short bursts of energy, we shouldn't expect early scribble activity to go on for more than a few minutes at a time. Later, when the child starts practicing making shapes and eventually naming his scribbles, he may work for longer (possibly 30 minutes or more). We should try not to interfere with the scribbling process by stopping the child in the middle of it. Sometimes a scribble looks exciting to us (or we read something into it) and we may want to stop the child before he "messes it up." Even though it might be tempting to try and rescue the drawing, it is best to let the child finish the scribble when he is ready to. He doesn't know anything about art and he doesn't really care what the final drawing looks like.

Feedback

Children this age will scribble with anything they can get their hands on (a lipstick, chocolate pudding, or applesauce are frequent favorites). The scribbler is very excited about the idea that the drawn line stands out on the page. White drawing paper and dark felt-tip markers or crayons (with the paper peeled off) can be used effectively because the images the child makes will stand out more clearly. Scribblers get just as surprised and excited about their drawings as we do, and they can't see them if there are words or designs on the paper.

No matter what developmental stage the child is in, he still wants and needs praise. Encouraging words will always comfort and support the young child as he goes about his business of playful exploration. Once the child has begun making shapes like circles, we can reinforce the concept by pointing to other objects in the room that are also circular. Later, when he starts naming his scribbles, he will probably tell a little story about them. He might make some free-flowing lines and shapes and then say, "This is you, mom." We can help the child take the idea even further by asking questions like "Where am I going? What am I wearing? What am I doing?"

Whenever possible, we should try to date the drawings and also write down whatever the child says about them on the back of the paper. This is a simple but effective way to chronicle children's artistic and cognitive development, not only for ourselves, but for them. As they mature, many children enjoy reflecting on their earlier work. By saving and cherishing their work, we give them the message that their creations are valid and meaningful. After the child is done with a scribbling session, we should display some of the drawings on the refrigerator or any place where the child can see them. The rest can be stored in a folder. Some of these special paintings and stories (and the later ones we collect) can one day be made into an "art album" for our children when they are older. In this way, creativity is established as a family legacy.

Besides scribbling, art projects for very young children can include: play dough, collage, painting, and finger-painting prints (see Chapter 5).

Working with Preschematics (4-7 Years Old)

As scribbles evolve into conscious, discernible drawings, the child enters into a very exciting and productive time in her artistic development. Artwork is created spontaneously, with lines and forms turning magically into recognizable objects. Images are exaggerated and distorted and color and spatial arrangements are chosen randomly. The child may draw whimsical fantasy creatures such as a purple cat who floats above ground and carries an umbrella.

She is not concerned about what art should be or how to make things "correctly." The way she draws is emotionally connected to the way she experiences or imagines the world. Her pictures come out of a rich fantasy life that transcends the adult version of reality. She creates images that are personally important to her and she draws things the way she feels them. Children this age are very proud of their artwork and they like to talk about it. Even without much encouragement, most young children will continue making highly inventive artwork, at least until they pass through the *Preschematic Stage*.

Feedback

Even though artmaking is something that the young child may do naturally (and prodigously), she still deserves praise and support for her efforts. When the child shows us her artwork, it is best not to make assumptions about its content before asking her about the painting. Neglecting to ask a child about her work before commenting on it may result in some confused and hurt feelings. The adult may say something to the child like "I love that tree and the big dog." But the child may react with an annoyed expression on her face. She might say, "That's *not* a tree, it's a giant cactus plant and that's *not* a dog, it's a tiger." Although the adult tried to be supportive, he missed, and the result was a child who felt misunderstood.

Rather than telling the child what *we* think the painting is about, we should simply ask her how she created it. Questions like "What colors did you mix to get this beautiful reddish color?" or "What other materials did you use in your painting?" give the child a chance to tell us about some of the steps she went through in order to create her work. As she explains the way her painting evolved, she becomes an expert by telling us how she made it all happen. But it is important to note that if the child does not want to talk about her painting, we should never force the issue or make her feel that she has to somehow justify her work with words.

One of the reasons artmaking is such a universal activity is that it serves important emotional, psychological, and cognitive functions throughout life. During this age and beyond, children may be using art to work out feelings about things of which they are aware, but do not yet understand. Even though the child may not have the vocabulary or the intellectual sophistication to talk about certain conflicts and fears, she is still aware of them. In her own way, she is taking them in. When we look at young children's drawings and see figures that look mad, sick, surprised, sad, mean, or threatening, first we can ask the child to tell us something about each of the characters. We can try to learn more about their significance by asking questions like "Where is that person going? How old is she? Where does she live? Why does she look sad? Does she feel sick? Is she mad? Why is she wearing boots and a hat? Is it going to rain? Where are her mommy and daddy? If she could talk right now, what would she say?" To gain more insight into the child's emotional life, we can also suggest that she use puppets to create plays and act out different roles. (See Chapter 5 for instructions on how to make puppets.)

Children should also be encouraged to use art as an emotional resource in case of an immediate crisis, such as the loss of a loved one, or other kinds of acute traumas. For example, when a child is dealing with the death of someone close to her, we can suggest that she create a book of drawings, collages, photos, poems, and/or stories about the person or pet. A project like this can help the child mourn the loss by giving her a focal point where she can process her feelings. Even at a young age, the child is trying to understand the cycle of life and that means, eventually, coming to grips with mortality. While death may symbolize the ultimate loss of control, making art can, metaphorically, be a way to try and reclaim some sense of order.

Suggested projects for 4–7 year olds include: painting, printing, clay, collage, crayon/watercolor resist, papier maché, and sculpture (see Chapter 5).

Working with Schematics (7-9 Years Old)

The child has gone from drawing what he experiences or imagines to drawing what he knows. Artmaking is no longer about the way the world feels to the child, but about the way he understands it. The development of a schema means that the child creates visual symbols that he repeats and refines. The symbol for the schema is determined by how the child connects emotionally and conceptually to an object. For his work to remain creative, the child needs to keep the schema flexible.

But some children have inflexible schemas that remain static and fixed. Images such as rainbows, hearts, smiley faces, rocket ships, lollipop flowers, and curvy-shaped clouds are examples of stereotypic schemas that sometimes get used repeatedly, especially when a child feels unsure about his art ability. When children say they don't know what to draw, they will frequently resort to these familiar kinds of images because they are safe and essentially foolproof. (You can hardly get a lollipop flower "wrong.")

When we look at some of these rigid schemas, and even some of the more personal ones, we wonder what happened to the free-flowing and expressive paintings that were apparent only a year or so before.

One answer might be that for some children, art has become more self-conscious than it used to be (and maybe less enjoyable). During this stage, the child is moving away from expressionistic art and more toward literalism. But, by creating schemas that show us what he knows, he is also revealing a lot about his experiences and how he relates to them.

Children's schemas will differ tremendously, depending on sociological, economic, cultural, and psychological factors. Children who have contact with farm animals or go to the zoo frequently or have pets may create elaborate schemas for animals. Similarly, children who are exposed to diverse landscapes like forests, rivers, and mountains (either through books or travel) may have more complex schemas for images connected to nature. But children who are deprived of extracurricular educational programs and rich cultural and intellectual experiences will have less resources to draw from. They may remain attached to flat and stereotypic schemas for the comfort of their familiarity. We should know that just because some of these children repeat prefabricated images for a period of time does not mean that they could not, if given the right opportunities, create highly expressive and original artwork.

Feedback

One of the ways that we can help children grow creatively is to encourage *difference* in ways that expand the child's perspective of the world. Even if the school culture emphasizes conformity, we can construct an environment, either in the individual classroom or at home, where independent thinking and originality are valued.

We can also help children establish a sense of confidence by supporting whatever effort they put out, no matter how minimal it might be. For instance, if a child is repeatedly drawing the same image like rainbows, we should still support the effort. When a child is that unsure about his potential, it is best to take off from the place that is most comfortable for him (in this case, the rainbows). At this point, if we tried to get him to draw horses, sports figures, or skyscrapers, it might be too threatening. In such a situation, encouraging the child to think differently about the rainbows might represent a starting point for more creative projects in the future. When we see the rainbow image over and over again, we can use any of the following comments and questions to encourage the child to experiment: "You really make good rainbows. Can you make a bigger one? Can you fill up the page with different color rainbows? Can you imagine someone flying on top of a rainbow? If you could create a rainbow sculpture that could float in the air, what would you make it with? What do you think a rainbow factory would look like?"

Although we should not draw for a child, we can always help him brainstorm for ideas. If he is truly at a loss and he asks us what to draw, we can ask him questions about his daily (and nightly) experiences. "Did you have an interesting dream last night? Was it scary? Was it funny? What did you see on the street today when you walked to school? Who did you sit with at lunch? What did you do at recess?" If these questions don't elicit a visual narrative, we could encourage the child to take any one of these daily events and put some fantasy into them. For instance, after we asked, "What did you see on the street today?" we could could follow it up with, "Why don't you draw something you wished you had seen on the street today?" or "What about doing a drawing that starts with a part of the dream you had and ends up somewhere you can't even imagine yet?" The best outcome from all of this prompting would be that the child shows *no* interest in any of our proposed ideas, but formulates his own project instead. After all, the point of these questions is to stimulate the child to come up with his own original ideas, not to have him follow ours.

Suggested art projects for 7–9 year olds include: drawing, painting, fabric-painting collage, string prints, glue prints, sculptures, clay, Styrofoam prints, and papier maché. (See Chapter 5 for other projects, suggestions, and art references for younger children.)

Working with Dawning Realists (9-12 Years Old)

The older child has not only become critically aware of herself in relation to her family, she is also aware of the world around her. She may even be thinking about (and dealing with) political and social issues such as racism, violence, the environment, sexism, poverty, and hunger. Because she has become more critical of her own family and other adults in positions of authority, her sense of justice has become heightened. She challenges her parents and others about what she thinks is unfair.

The physical changes in her body might be causing her much anguish and insecurity. Fashion magazines and the media are still using the standard version of blonde, blue-eyed, ultra-thin women and athletic-looking, tall men as archetypes of *beauty*. Since this Eurocentric model blatantly discounts ethnic diversity and differences in body type, the older child who doesn't fit in (and who does?) will undoubtedly feel insecure. Many older children react to all of this attention on physical perfection by becoming depressed, feeling inferior, and losing confidence in themselves. Preteens, especially girls, may become overly involved with their weight. Eventually, some of them may end up developing eating disorders such as anorexia or bulimia.

The drawings of children this age reflect the socially-charged and media-driven stereotypes that have become so much a part of their lives. Whether older children are aware of it or not, pop culture has influenced the way they see and think about the world. Media images have idealized, sanitized, and slenderized the human body. Not surprisingly, drawings of figures often depict girls looking like Barbie dolls and boys looking like He-Man action figures. But even as the older child is practicing new ways of drawing and trying to figure out how she wants to represent herself and the rest of the world, she will occasionally return to the old and sometimes more comfortable schema of a younger, more sexually neutral person in order to express an idea or present a particular concept.

Feedback

For the preteen, making art can be an important way to assemble her perceptions about the world. As she moves away from childhood, she begins to look for an identity. She may wonder, "Who am I? What do I believe in? How am I different from my family?" and "What kind of a world am I growing up in?" Creating art may give her a chance to work out her feelings about getting older and dealing with issues that are not always easy to understand. Because older children are just beginning to separate their own ideas from those of their parents, they can sometimes become rigid about what they perceive as the one and only "right" way to do something. Art projects that involve brainstorming and creative thinking can help the older child see things in a broader way and take on new approaches to problem-solving.

But before we can even begin working with this age group, we have to start with the premise that children of all ages have important things to tell us, and they don't always use words. There is nothing that will turn off a preteen faster than being treated in a dismissive or condescending way. Children/adolescents have feelings, opinions, criticisms, and observations about the world that need to be listened to and validated. We may not agree with everything they say, but we need to take their experiences and ideas seriously. Parents and teachers should remember that the older child is just beginning to establish herself as her own person. Just because she pushes us away a little bit (or a lot) should not be a reason to withhold praise and support. In fact, that is the opposite of what we should do. Throughout the preteen years and the turbulent years that accompany adolescence, she needs praise and support as much as she ever did.

Suggested projects for 9-12 year olds include: drawing (especially contours), linoleum prints, collage prints, monotypes, string-print box sculptures, found object sculptures, self-portrait/memory box sculptures, painting, papier maché, plasticine, and mixed-media collage. (See Chapter 5 for other projects, suggestions, and art references for older children.)

Working with Pseudo-Naturalists (12-14 Years Old)

The age between 12 and 14 is the period when young adolescents begin to search for self. They start redefining themselves in a way that is separate and different from their parents and even their peers. Although they are still spending a lot of time in groups, some of them are becoming interested in dating. In addition, some combination of sex, drugs, drinking, parties, popular music, and risk-taking have become a pervasive part of the youth culture. The young adolescent has moved away from the perceived safety net of childhood and is on an uncharted journey filled with excitement and temptation. But she may also be painfully self-conscious and insecure. As parents and teachers, we often feel like we are watching from the sidelines, rooting for our teens, worrying about them, and desperately seeking to believe that everything will turn out all right.

Because they are going through a rapid and awkward period of sexual maturation, the artwork of many young adolescents may show a fascination, or even a preoccupation, with the physical body. At this age, it is not unusual to see figurative drawings with truncated body parts, exaggerated sexual characteristics, grotesque facial features, and even odd physical deformities, sometimes integrated into the same work of art. Although these images might look a little strange or even disturbing to some of us, this kind of art expression is actually a good way for the young teen to explore the parameters of the physical body, and that includes its sexual aspects. By using art to play with the human form, distorting and manipulating it, and sometimes visually depicting violent scenes (as reflected in the culture), the young teen may be touching on some intensely personal concerns. Just as younger children acted out their anxieties through drawings of super-heroes and bad guys, warriors and dragons, angels and devils, or other themes of good and evil, young teens may also use art to contend with their projected fears and insecurities.

Feedback

As parents and teachers, many of us worry that we are losing connection with our young adolescents. We don't know as much about what they are thinking or feeling because they don't let us into their lives the way they used to. Young teens are figuring out how they want to be seen and known in the world. As such, they seek more privacy and separation from us than they did before. At this stage, most adolescents want as little supervision as possible, and that includes artmaking. For the most part, only a small group of young teenagers make art in art classes. The majority of teens do not take high school art classes, either because they don't have the opportunity or because they feel intimidated and artistically inadequate. Some teens, reflecting prevailing adult values regarding art in education, may not even think of art as being important. But no matter what students consciously think about art, or about their perceived ability as *artists*, most of them end up making it anyway in the form of doodles.

Doodles and other types of process-oriented artwork can be generated by students through sketchbooks that can be used to observe the world, chronicle everyday experiences, and tap into the imagination. Because some young teens are creating drawings that they are reluctant to share, the book may take on a private or "secret" quality. It is not a good idea for adults to look at it without asking first because teenagers (like adults) need to feel that their personal space is being respected. But, when adolescents do share their work with us, we should refrain from making declarations about what we think is appropriate or not appropriate to draw. No matter what the subject matter is, even if we find it shocking or objectionable, drawings should never be censored or belittled. Art expression can be a helpful emotional and psychological outlet for the teen.

Suggested project ideas for young adolescents include: drawing, painting, clay, collage, plasticine, papier maché, sculpture, and print-making. (See Chapter 6 for other projects, suggestions, and art references for young adolescents.)

Working with Adolescent Artists (14-17 Years Old)

The search for self-identity intensifies at the end of adolescence. Because the adolescent is in a constant struggle to shed childhood constraints and chart a way into adult territory, she may not be the easiest person to live with. For many families, the adolescent years feel like everything is turning upside-down. The structure of home life starts shifting as the teenager spends less time with the family and becomes more emotionally inaccessible. Both the parent and the adolescent experience confusion, loss, anger, and frustration as the teenager tries to push boundaries on all levels. These strong emotions on both sides often end up in a no-win power struggle with the parents trying to hold on to rules that just don't seem to work anymore.

As the teenager becomes more independent, she starts making decisions on her own. She can learn to drive a car, get a part-time job, plan trips, and make choices about her social life. She may be thinking about applying to college and living away from home. While she wonders, "What do I want to be when I grow up?" she is still trying to figure out what "growing up" means. She remains self-conscious about her appearance and she's concerned about what other people think of her. As she moves closer to adulthood, she is filled with thoughts of impending liberation, but also with anxiety and self-doubt.

Sadly, by the time children reach adolescence, many of them have lost touch with the freewheeling process of artmaking. But, many teenagers are still engaged daily in certain types of art experiences

such as experimenting with clothing and make-up and using their bodies to explore identity. Through new fashion styles, accessories, body
piercing, tattooing, and hairstyles, many teens explore individuality
and test the limits of social acceptability.

Whether the teenager has continued making art throughout childhood or not, she can accumulate drawing skills rapidly if she suddenly gets motivated to do so. If art is a subject that she finds meaningful,
she may spend long periods of uninterrupted time, in a school environment or on her own, learning techniques and mastering new materials. Teenagers enjoy artistic experimentation, and their tastes are
eclectic.

Feedback

The artistic teenager has become even more of an introspective
observer than she was before. She should continue keeping a process-
oriented sketchbook or a lightweight camera with her whenever possible. Teachers can suggest that the student photograph or draw one
particular theme for a few weeks at a time. Examples are billboards,
buildings, houses, stores, parks, cars, trees, or people. Students could
also write verbal descriptions of objects and share their writings with
the class. Art projects could be generated through these alone.
Another idea that can be a lot of fun is for students to tape-record a
three-minute conversation with someone (but only with their permis-
sion), and bring the tape in for the class to hear. Students could then
make up a visual story about the people who were talking. These kinds
of off-beat art experiences give teens a chance to engage in creative
play (something they may not do enough of). Eventually, this constructive fooling around may lead to other interesting ideas and self-
generating projects.

Sometimes teenage students, especially those who have been drawing on their own for a while, have created a highly individualized style
of artmaking. These students may not want to follow the rest of the
class. They may be involved with graffiti art, cartooning, designing letters or patterns, creating imaginary characters, or making up surreal
scenarios. Often their artwork represents a theme or an unresolved
issue that is especially meaningful for them. The teen does not want to
let that style or theme go and she shouldn't have to. While it is impor-

tant that teens get exposure to different kinds of media (such as print-making, clay, sculpture, and collage), and drawing techniques (such as blind contours, observational, automatic, modelled, and gesture draw-ings), students shouldn't feel pressured to join in on class projects if their own work interests them more.

With older adolescents, the sketchbook continues to be a source of creative investigation and a way to access intuitive and subconscious material. Drawings are important in and of themselves and they often serve as the impetus for future art projects. Just as scribbles were a barometer for the toddler's cognitive development, drawings and doo-dles in this phase tell us much about what concerns the adolescent. The drawings may open a window into a private world that reveals what the teen considers "cool," what she thinks is beautiful, what makes her sad, what she fantasizes about, and what she fears.

The teenager is still figuring out how she should look, how she should act, and how she wants to be seen by others. She may be deal-ing with a number of personal problems and angst-driven issues that she doesn't like to talk about. Although she may want to be noticed, she does not want to be judged. Adults must be aware that it is not easy for teens to let them into their creative and very personal universe. If teenagers are offering to share their thoughts, feelings, and ideas with us, through the medium of art, we should feel privileged to be a part of their private world. In showing us her art projects, the teenager needs to feel that she is on emotionally safe ground. One of the ways we can honor that need is to be nonjudgemental and enthusiastic about her efforts. Still, we can ask sensitive but provocative questions about her work. (See Chapter 6, under "Individual Needs, Feedback, and the Creative Process," for a further discussion of ways to support teenage artwork and for other projects, suggestions, and art references for adolescents.)

Art projects for older adolescents include painting, drawing, papier maché, sculpture, clay, plasticine, collage, mixed-media work, and printmaking such as monotype. The next chapter looks at art projects for younger children from ages 2 to 12.

Chapter 5
ART PROJECTS FOR CHILDREN AGES 2 TO 12

FINDING A PLACE TO MAKE ART

Before we introduce specific projects for children, we need to set up an environment where artmaking can happen. Most of us do not have a formal art studio for our children to work in, nor do we necessarily have a designated room in the house that can be used for making art. But, in order to provide an atmosphere where creative work can happen, we need a space where children can feel free to make a productive mess. Clean-up is easy with water-based materials and even young children can help. Eventually, they will think of it as a natural part of the art experience.

During nice weather, we can work with children outside at a picnic table or on the grass, provided that we cover the ground with something flat so that we have a smooth area to work on. But during the cold months of the year, we need a special place where children can create things. A corner of the child's room, the hallway, even a small section of the family room (best if uncarpeted), can be turned into a temporary studio. If you use the dining room or the kitchen, remember to keep all art materials far away from any food source.

When setting up for an art project, it is best to work on a long, smooth surface, like a table. If using a household table is not an option, an alternative is a sturdy fold-up table or sheets of heavy cardboard placed on the floor, covered with newspapers. In thinking about the best space for artmaking, we should look for a room with good ventilation and easy access to a sink. Most projects require water whether we work with clay, paint, ink, papier maché, or other materials. Also, children need water to help clean up spills and wash their hands after using art materials.

Buying and Storing Art Supplies

The best quality and selection of art supplies can usually be found in art supply stores. But some stationery stores, drug stores, department stores, and even supermarkets carry general art supplies such as glue sticks, white glue, crayons, construction paper, scissors, and drawing paper. When looking for art supplies for children, we should always buy products that are safe to use. (Check the *Appendix*–"Art Materials and Safety Information.")

One way to keep supplies organized is in a portable kitchen cart with storage shelves. That way, supplies can be moved from room to room, wherever artmaking happens. Another way to store materials is in shoe boxes or in large plastic containers sold at stationery or hardware stores that are designed to hold pencils, paints, glues, and other miscellaneous items. As mentioned in Chapter 4, student artwork should be saved, dated, and placed in a portfolio. The portfolio and drawing paper can be kept together in a closet or even under a bed.

Working Together: The Parent/Teacher Role

"Working together" means different things to us and our children at different stages in our lives. When children are younger, we are more involved with their projects because they need more help. Some of us may even paint with them, working side by side. But, as discussed in Chapter 1, sometimes creating art simultaneously with young children can have a negative effect. In our enthusiasm to help our child, we might, unknowingly, set up a competitive edge. If a parent draws a tree and then says, "There, see how I do it? Now you can make your own," the child may not only try to emulate the adult, but he may also feel that his tree is inferior. If the child asks us to draw the tree for him, we should tell him that we can't do that because we know that he sees and knows the tree in a different way than we do. We can explain what we mean by saying something like, "Drawing for someone is like speaking for him, putting words in his mouth, or even thinking for him." Children need to know that it is a *good* thing that we all see the world differently and that many adults not only appreciate and admire children's art, but also find it inspirational. The underlying issue here is that children need a chance to develop their *own* unique visual language. They can't do that if we, even inadvertently, try to mold their vision.

The main function of making art concurrently with young children should be to stimulate the child's interest in his own art or to help with some technical or mechanical aspect of the child's project. Examples would be mixing colors, kneading clay, or demonstrating new techniques, such as printing or papier maché. Working together with older children and adolescents may mean providing materials, helping to facilitate projects, and setting up an environment where creative work can happen. But regardless of whether we are working with young children or adolescents, art sessions should be noncompetitive in every way and the center of attention should always stay on the child/adolescent and never on the adult. I believe that the most productive role for a parent or teacher in art sessions is one of supervisor (when needed), supporter, stimulator, nurturer, and respectful collaborator.

Individual Needs, Feedback, and the Creative Process

Another important aspect of working together is being sensitive to the individual needs of the child. Everyone approaches the art experience differently. Sometimes the older child wants to participate in art-making, but he feels uncomfortable. Maybe he's afraid that he might "fail" and he can't think of what to do. He may not like the projects we suggest or he may secretly think that he doesn't have the "skill" to try out something new. When this happens, it is always helpful to have a few extra supplies around to stimulate and encourage new ideas. A box of scraps consisting of things like ripped-up and discarded road maps; old calendars; cut-out pictures from magazines; colored, patterned, tissue, or textured paper; fabric and wallpaper swatches; glue sticks; and watercolor crayons should be kept on hand.

If the child goes through the box and still can't think of what to do, we should bring the focus back to the pure elements of art process—*play and discovery*. The following questions and comments may stimulate ideas: "What if you put a few paints on a palette and then closed your eyes, and mixed up any two colors that your brush comes in contact with? I wonder what colors you could make. What if you painted a few colors on the paper and then ripped it into different shapes for a collage? What if you poured black ink on white paper and then moved the paper up and down, letting the paint run all over the edges? I bet you could see a lot of images in the shapes that the dripping ink makes. Maybe you could turn the shapes into animals, robots, or creatures from another planet." After playing around with ideas, we could put out even more colors. The child could mix and paint, using large and small brushes, sticks, or cut-up sponges. Also, if the adult has access to a computer, it would be interesting for the child to have some of his artwork scanned. By using various software applications, with our help (if he needs it), he can manipulate the images even further. He can also look at other children's artwork from around the world on the Internet. The child may want to talk about some of these paintings and even make up stories about them.

While this chapter suggests art projects for younger children, Chapter 6 suggests art projects for adolescents from ages 12 to 17. The art projects in both of these chapters are designed for each specific stage of artistic development from scribbling to adolescent art. But since stages of artistic development can overlap, many of the projects are appropriate for other age groups, too. Projects for all of the stages are meant to be process-oriented and the focus should stay on the act of creating, not producing a product. Children should always be made to feel that they are special and that their artwork is an extention of their uniqueness. The criterion for "success" is not how the product looks, but what the art experience brings to the child/adolescent. If the student had fun doing it, if he learned something from it, and if he felt good about himself afterwards, the project was successful. One of the ways we can insure success is for projects to be open-ended so that the student feels that there are many different ways to approach artmaking. The projects are not meant to be strictly followed, but to serve as a catalyst to create original art. Ultimately, successful art experiences accumulate and help to reinforce self-confidence, problem-solving skills, and self-esteem.

Planning, Brainstorming, and Cleaning Up

When working with very young children, we need to be especially flexible. Some sessions may last only a few minutes while others can go on for much longer periods. The young child is constantly exploring things, and making art is no exception. Ripping the paper, spilling the paint, stepping in it, or making hand prints on the walls are all a part of discovering new art materials. To prevent an overload of creative chaos, projects need to be planned carefully, but should be changed, or stopped, on the spot if they are not working. All projects need maximum supervision and they should be ended promptly when the child seems restless. If a very young child's attention begins to wander, he will let us know by simply playing with something else, running around the room in a burst of energy, or just getting up and walking away.

As the child gets older and his attention span lengthens, it will become clear that the project is not working for him when, after a few minutes, he says, "I'm finished." When that happens, we know that he is bored, frustrated, or at a loss for what to do next. At that point, we can offer some new paints or mixed media, like watercolors, wax crayons, and collage, for him to use and suggest that he fill up the entire paper with colors and pasted shapes. But if that doesn't work, we may need to change the project to something else, like clay, because that might suit him better.

Regardless of age, students enjoy working in an organized environment where they can create things. Sometimes playing mellow jazz or classical music tapes can help to establish a peaceful and calming atmosphere that invites quiet work. The sessions can begin by looking over artwork done in previous sessions or they can begin with an explanation of the project for that particular day. If students are working on more than one project at once, they should be able to choose the project that interests them the most, even if it is not the one that everyone else is working on. There are times when it may be best to put away problematic projects and then return to them at a much later date, hopefully, with a new perspective. If there is enough time at the end of a session, students can share ideas and talk about their own work and the work of others.

Clean-up should be a simple and routine affair with children washing their hands at the sink and, when possible, helping to throw away paint palettes, unusable scraps, and old newspapers. Have some all-natural liquid hand soap at the sink, and keep plenty of paper towels around. Put a few drops of unscented, all-natural dish-washing liquid in a plastic spray bottle of water for cleaning the table and wiping up spills. Clean-up may be easier in some cases if students, especially young children, wear an old shirt or a "smock" over their clothes while they work.

Scribblers (2 or Younger–4 Years Old)

Drawing—You will need: drawing paper, felt-tip markers, and water-based or wax crayons. When working with very young children, make sure that drawing tools do not have sharp points. Also, crayons are easier for scribblers to use if the paper is peeled off.

Since scribblers love to make marks, we should have a special crayon box filled with materials for them to use. Wax and water-based crayons or thick, dark-colored, water-based, felt-tip markers work well with children this age. Plain white paper or all-purpose, light-colored drawing paper shows off the scribbles best (see Figures 26 & 27).

*Figure 26 - **Scribblers**:* Drawing by a 3-year-old child. This child practiced making letter scribbles, over and over, especially "A" and "N" (It may not be a total surprise to learn that the child's name started with an "A"). After she made a few of these scribbles, she gathered them all around her and pretended to read. Eventually her mom and dad compiled a bunch of these drawings and stapled them into a "book" with her name on it.

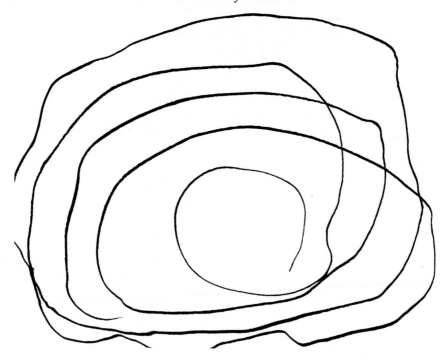

*Figure 27 - **Scribblers**:* Circle Scribble by a 3-year-old child. This scribbler was having a lot of fun moving his arm in big, sweeping motions and making this broad maze of circular shapes.

Play Dough—You will need: play dough, paint, and glue (optional).

Because play dough is so tactile and easy to use, it is a favorite material for very young children. Children play by rolling it, pounding it, punching it, making holes in it with their fingers or sticks, cutting it, breaking it into pieces, making balls out of it, and doing anything else to it they can possibly think of. Because it is so malleable, they can create lots of shapes. The shapes can easily be changed, added to, or subtracted from. But, pieces don't usually last indefinitely because play dough is not considered permanent. Eventually it may crumble and fall apart. When the child is finished with a play dough sculpture, it can be painted and displayed. We can either buy ready-made Play-Doh in the store or we can make our own uncooked recipe from natural ingredients. Try this one: *2¹/₂ cups flour, ¹/₂ cup salt, 1 tablespoon creme of tartar, 3 tablespoons vegetable oil, 1¹/₂ cups hot water, and a few drops of food coloring. Combine oil, water, and food coloring in one bowl. Put dry ingredients in another. Pour liquid into dry ingredients. Mix thoroughly, knead, and play. (Add more flour if the mixture is too wet.) If there is any dough left, put it in a plastic food bag and store it in the refrigerator. For best consistency, take the play dough out of the refrigerator for about an hour before using it again.*

Homemade play dough may take as long as a week to thoroughly dry. Once it has finally dried, try covering it with a layer of diluted white glue. If you decide to paint it (optional), wait until the glue dries completely. The glue might help to stabilize and strengthen the piece.

Ripped Paper Collage—You will need: a piece of cardboard, collage scraps, and glue sticks.

Since children at this age love to rip things apart and they are capable of using nontoxic glue sticks, collage can be a good medium for them to try. Adults can provide cut-up papers that may interest the child, such as: colored or patterned papers, the child's own scribbles, wrapping paper, or magazine pictures. The scraps can be put in a box and the children can choose the ones they like. They can change the original shapes by ripping them and, with our help, pasting the back of the shapes onto a piece of heavy paper or cardboard (see Figure 28).

*Figure 28 - **Scribblers**:* Ripped Paper Collage by a 3½-year-old child. Using his own drawing scraps and other ripped-up pieces of paper, the child made this collage on cardboard. He needed a little help getting enough glue on the back of the scraps to make the paper stick.

Note: After all collages are finished, they should be covered with a piece of plexiglass and a heavy board, for a few hours or overnight, to prevent warping.

Painting—You will need: water-based paint, paintbrushes, and paper.

Painting with very young children can either be done on the floor (covered with newspapers), a long table, or an easel. For preschoolers, working at an easel can feel "grown up" and special. A real benefit of the easel is that it offers children a greater range of arm movement than they would have if they worked at a small table, especially if it were crowded with other children. When using an easel, children also seem delighted and surprised to see how the paint drips down the paper in beautiful and unpredictable ways. Also, easels usually have special holders for individual paint containers, so that the mechanics of painting and mixing become a little more controlled. For mixing on the floor or a table, use either an old muffin tin or a small piece of plexiglass covered with tin foil for a palette.

Although painting with scribblers is a messy, fast-paced experience, it is also fascinating, even exhilarating, to watch. A lot of supervision is needed and it is best not to have too many children painting at the same time. Diluted tempera paint or diluted water-based printing inks should be placed in small plastic bowls and one brush can be provided for each color. (Keep color choices to a minimum.) Brushes should be kept where children can easily reach them. Although painting for scribblers is mostly a sensory, kinesthetic, and exploratory experience, many children this age will give their paintings a name and sometimes even make up stories about them (see Figures 29 & 30).

*Figure 29 - **Scribblers***: Painting by a $2^{1}/_{2}$-year-old child. This child was making random marks and moving paint around the page when one of his playmates suddenly said, "Hey, that's a giraffe." At that point, the child put down his paintbrush and repeated the word "giraffe" a few times. Then, he smiled. He seemed to make a connection between what his friend said and the painting he was making. Although the child may not have even known what a giraffe was, he figured out that he must have "made something." Right after that, he pushed the painting aside and started a new one.

*Figure 30 - **Scribblers**:* Painting by a 3½-year-old child. Painting was a very intense experience for this child, who seemed mesmerized by the sensory activity of dunking his brush in the paint and adding more and more layers to the picture. He spent about 10 minutes on this painting before he suddenly dropped his paintbrush and said, "I'm done." Just as he was running off to play with something else, he looked back at his painting and said, "It's a giant rock."

Finger Painting Prints—*You will need: finger paints, plexiglass, paper and lots of paper towels.*

Note: This project will need extra supervision and a lot of cleaning up. But it's worth the mess because young children seem to like it so much.

Buy nontoxic finger paints in a stationery or art store. Put a large piece of plexiglass on the floor or on the table. The children will be painting directly on the plexiglass. If there are a few children working together, make sure that there is enough space between them so that they each have room to paint. Empty the finger paint jar into a plastic container large enough for children to insert their hands. Put smocks on the children if you have any. As they start to make hand prints, encourage them to think of different ways to use their hands as a tool for painting. They can try the side of the hand, individual fingers, fingertips, fingernails, knuckles, and so on. The paint can be rubbed off the plexiglass in certain areas with a makeshift tool like a small piece of cardboard or a moistened paper towel. The plexiglass can also be scratched with a finger or a blunt stick. Once the children have created the painting they want on the plexiglass, we can make a print of it. Simply lay a piece of ordinary drawing paper on top of the painting, and rub the back of it with overall hand pressure, the back of a spoon, a spatula, or a dry roller. After a few moments of rubbing, pull off the paper.

Preschematics (4-7 Years Old)

Drawing—You will need: drawing paper and one or more of the following—water-based crayons, wax crayons, different colored felt-tip markers, oil pastels.

During this period of rapid cognitive growth and prodigious artistic activity, we can encourage children's creative expression even more by providing interesting and varied opportunities for image-making. Because drawing helps children make sense of the world, they may do a lot of it at this age. Buying young children their own sketchbook (kept in a secure place) can make art activities even more special. As with scribble drawings, artwork may be accompanied by the child's short explanations or highly imaginative and sometimes very funny and charming little stories (see Figure 31). These comments and stories, which can be anything from a few words to a few sentences, are treasures that are too precious to lose or be forgotten. (See Chapter 4, under "Working with Scribblers" for a discussion of the importance of saving children's drawings and stories.)

*Figure 31 - **Preschematics:*** Drawing by a 4-year-old child. This family portrait is called, "My cat, daddy, me and mommy." When asked about the hat on the figure on the far right (her mom), the child said, "My mom wore that to her wedding." Notice that the child is holding hands with both of her parents. The line around all of them symbolizes their house.

Painting—You will need: paper, water-based paint, paintbrushes and lots of paper towels.

Diluted tempera or diluted water-based inks can be used in the same way as described for scribblers. Because younger children sometimes like to rotate their paper while they work, and they need space to make big gestures with their arms, it might be a good idea to paint on the floor. A table or an easel will also work well, as long as there is enough space between children. Since most children by age four are creating symbols that can be recognized by others, paintings at this stage begin to take on a narrative quality. Usually the child paints subjects that mean a lot to him, like his family or a pet. Painting sessions may last a little longer than they did with scribblers. After the child finishes his painting, he may want to talk about it (See Figures 32 & 33).

*Figure 32 - **Preschematics**:* Painting by a 4-year-old child. Before she started to paint, this child decided that she was going to create a person. But after fooling around with the paint for a while, she said, "It's not really a person and it's not even an animal. It's just a painting."

*Figure 33 - **Preschematics**:* Painting by a 6-year-old child. This child painted an interesting family portrait with himself on the left and his mom and dad in the middle. Dad is tallest and mom has on a skirt. His big brother and little sister are to the right of his dad. Even though all of the family members are standing in a row, it feels as if they are still moving, or just about to go somewhere. When asked where everyone was going, the child said, "We're just being busy."

Vegetable/Found Object Prints—You will need: a variety of hard vegetables like potatoes and peppers, some found objects, water-based paints, paintbrushes, paper, and a lot of paper towels.

Note: Children will need extra help with this project.

Vegetable prints can be made with any hard vegetable that has a smooth surface. Potatoes, peppers, turnips, and onions can be used effectively. Vegetables can be cut into triangles, circles, half-circles, squares, star shapes, or whatever else you can imagine. Paint is applied to one side of the vegetable and it is then stamped onto the paper. Cookie cutters, old potato mashers, the round end of a paper cup, and any object with a flat surface can also be used, in the same way as with the vegetables, to create varied shapes (see Figure 34).

*Figure 34 - **Preschematics:*** Vegetable/Found Object Print by a 4-year-old child. This print was made using potatoes, peppers, onions, the round end of a cup, and a cookie cutter. The child thought it was very funny that vegetables (usually a part of her dinner) could be used to make art. She enjoyed applying the paint to the vegetables and other found objects and then stamping them onto the paper.

Clay (playing and processing)–You will need: self-drying clay, a plastic cover for the table, newspapers or a piece of canvas to put on top of the plastic, a dish of water, a spray bottle filled with water, diluted white glue, a square piece of heavy board to put the sculpture on while it's drying, paints, a paintbrush, and (optional) collage materials.

Young children are more likely to play with the clay and stick things into it than they are to actually mold it. But, they really enjoy experimenting with this flexible medium. The free-form sculptures they make can be painted, collaged, and kept indefinitely. The easiest clay to use is the self-drying kind that comes in 5-pound boxes and does not have to be baked. (Check the *Appendix*–"Art Materials and Safety Information" to make sure that the brand you buy is safe for children.) When using clay, we should be aware of the fact that after it dries, it can crack or break. This happens primarily when unstable clay pieces are loosely stuck together or when the clay dries unevenly. Uneven drying results when some parts of the sculpture are too thick, while others are too thin. This imbalance can put stress on the clay and make it brittle. The following ideas may help to even out the drying process:

1. *Before the sculpture is totally dry, make small holes in the bottom or hollow it out.* After the sculpture is finished and well before it has dried, turn it over and hollow out the bottom with a measuring spoon. (Children can do this.) But, if you decide to make holes on the bottom instead, adults should take over because sharp utensils, such as the end of pointed scissors or a long nail, are needed. Holes should be about one-inch deep, but they may be less or more, depending on the size of the piece.

2. *Check for cracks, dry, and then cover with diluted white glue.* After the sculpture is finished, and while it is still wet or damp, check it over for cracks. Use water and your fingers to press unstable areas together. Smooth and rub parts of the surface in order to close up all of the cracks. After the sculpture is totally dry, brush diluted white glue over the whole thing. This may help to protect the clay and even prevent some of the more delicate pieces from breaking off. After the glue has dried, the sculpture can be painted and/or collaged.

3. *Slow down and even out the drying process.* If one section of the sculpture is very thin, mist that area with water so that it doesn't dry before the rest of the sculpture. Also, after the sculpture is finished, cover it loosely with a large plastic food bag, allowing for air to come up the sides.

To keep the clay moist, a small pan of water or a spray bottle filled with water should be kept near the art table in case it is needed. When working with young children, give them plenty of time to explore the clay. They need to process and manipulate it before figuring out what, if anything, to do next. Eventually, they may discover what they want to make out of it or they may stop playing with it when they notice that they already *have* made something out of it. Some ways to work with clay involve pinching, rolling, fingering, squeezing, flattening, patting, pounding, tearing, cutting, poking, stamping, or adding and taking away. If the child is still not finished at the end of the session, you can cover the sculpture tightly with plastic wrap and moisten it before the child uses it again. An important role for the adult during all of this frenetic activity is to try to make sure that the child's product is stable and will not fall apart.

After children have spent a while playing with the clay, you can bring out a box of materials ready for them to stick in their sculptures. Examples are toothpicks, cut-up scraps of corrugated cardboard, popsicle sticks, small twigs, broken combs, pipe cleaners, cut-up Styrofoam scraps, feathers, thin wood scraps, and drinking straws. Children can make wonderful snake-like creatures, plant forms, or pretend city environments out of clay pieces and recycled materials.

Note: Children should rinse their hands in a separate bucket before washing at the sink because clay can clog the drain. Empty the bucket of muddy water outside in the yard.

Mixed Paper Collage—You will need: paper scraps, glue, and a board.

Put magazine scraps, colored paper pieces, origami paper, gift wrapping scraps, transparent colored tissue paper (cut into pieces), and any other kinds of interesting paper into a box. Children can look through the box and rip or cut shapes out of anything they want to. They will need lots of glue and a strong surface like cardboard to paste on. Give them the colored tissue paper after they have glued down other solid paper shapes. The tissue paper transparencies will show up better that way.

Crayon/Watercolor Resist—You will need: ordinary wax crayons or oil pastels, watercolors, a paintbrush, and paper.

Using a lot of hand pressure to make very dark marks, children create drawings with wax crayons or oil pastels. After the drawing is completed, the child can choose one shade of transparent watercolor to paint over the entire drawing. This process is fun for the child because he enjoys watching the way the wax resists the water-based paint. The visual effects of the two media together are very appealing. (One is thick, dense, and heavy while the other is light, airy, and transparent.)

Papier Maché Puppets—You will need: wooden dowels, newspapers, glue, wire, masking tape, paint, paintbrushes, fabric scraps, and other collage materials.

Note: Children will need special help with this project, especially with making and applying the papier maché.

Papier maché can be made by cutting thin strips of newsprint or newspapers and dipping them in a bowl of diluted white glue. The glue strips are then wrapped around the structure of the sculpture. The structure or skeleton of the sculpture is called an *armature*. The armature can be made of wire, cardboard boxes, wood, or anything else that can make up the sculpture's foundation.

The following steps describe one way of making papier maché puppets:

1. Get a 6" wooden dowel, about $1/4$"–$1/2$" thick. Dowels can be bought at the hardware store.

2. Buy thin armature wire (at an art store) and wrap some of it around the top part of the dowel.

3. Make a sphere shape with the wire so that the wire and the dowel together look like a Tootsie Roll Pop.

4. Roll up newspapers into a small ball and stuff the ball inside the wire sphere to make a head. You may need to secure the ball with tape.

5. If you want the puppet to hang from the wall, flatten the back of the head and build out from the front of it. In order to make a hook, stick a paper clip into the flattened back of the newspaper ball while the papier maché is still wet. If you do not want the sculpture to hang from the wall, round out the back of the Tootsie Roll Pop shape and leave the clip out.

6. A face can be made by building shapes with the wet paper, painting directly on the round part of the ball, or by using precut collage images of eyes, noses, and mouths and just pasting them on.

7. Continue painting and collaging. Clothing scraps can be wrapped around the dowel to look like a cape. Yarn, fabric materials, cotton balls, paint, or anything else you can think of can be used for the hair or to make a hat.

Found Object Box Sculpture—You will need: a small piece of wood for the base, packaging boxes of varying sizes, cut-up pieces from a paper towel roll, glue, masking tape, wood scraps or toy blocks, collage materials, and paint.

Note: Children will need extra help with this project, especially with making and applying papier maché.

Small cardboard boxes, such as tea, cookie, and toothpaste boxes, can be glued together with pieces of scrap wood, old toy blocks, cut-up paper towel rolls, and other recycled materials to make imaginative sculptures. Also, packaging boxes in different shapes can be purchased inexpensively at the stationery store. Students of all ages can make fantasy machines, buildings, robots, people, animals, or whatever else they can think of. A piece of plywood, approximately 5"x 5", can be used for a base. The following steps describe one way to make a found object sculpture:

1. First, glue the cardboard boxes, wood scraps, and other found objects to the wooden base. Rounded shapes such as paper towel rolls will need to be taped to the boxes with masking tape or packaging tape. Make sure that the structure is stable and will not topple over.

2. Then, you can papier maché the entire structure, including the base.

3. Once the papier maché has dried, it is ready to paint. Collage elements such as magazine pictures, fabrics, feathers, strings, and colored paper can be added later. Making these sculptures often generates animated discussions, and even written stories, about objects or creatures that have magical powers (see Figure 35).

*Figure 35 - **Preschematics**:* Found Object Box Sculpture by a 6-year-old child. This sculpture was made by pasting a box and pieces of a paper towel roll to a wooden base. After all of the objects dried, the sculpture was covered entirely with papier maché and then painted. The project takes at least two sessions to complete. While this child was working on his sculpture, one of his friends asked him what he was making. He turned to him incredulously and asked, "How can I tell until it's done?" When the piece was finished, the child looked at it for a while. Finally, he announced, "It's a Fertilizer Maker."

Schematics (7-9 Years Old)

Drawing—You will need: paper and one or more of the following— black tempera paint and paintbrushes, black felt-tip markers, china markers, conté crayons, oil pastels, charcoal pencils or charcoal sticks, and any other assorted drawing tools that can be used to make marks.

After the age of 7 or so, most children are more self-conscious about their drawings. The following kinds of drawing projects can loosen students up and keep drawing a playful activity:

Automatic Drawings start out with the student making a spontaneous scribble. The student then reacts to the scribble by looking for something else in it and developing a new, more complex image. *Contour Drawings* are expressive line drawings that outline the edge of a form. They do not include modelling, shadows, or shading. In order to create a contour drawing, students need to look intensely at the subject. It helps to pretend to be touching the edge of it. Students are encouraged to slowly drag their drawing tools across the paper, rather than make quick sketchy movements with their hands (see Figure 36). *Blind Contour Drawings* are contour drawings with the added requirement that, while the drawing tool is moving, the student tries to look only at the model or the object she is drawing and not at her paper (see Figure 37). *Cut Out Contour Collages* are contour drawings using scissors instead of a pencil. After the shapes are cut out, they are pasted to another sheet of paper. *Imaginary Drawings* are drawings that incorporate dreams, memories, ideas, fantasies, pretend characters, adventure scenarios, doodles, designs, or anything that relies on imagination, and not direct observation.

*Figure 36 - **Schematics**:* Contour Drawing by an 8-year-old child. In this contour drawing, students were asked to put three figures on a page. The use of black ink and paintbrushes, rather than pencil, encouraged these fluid and expressive lines. Because the paint is harder to control, it keeps the drawing loose. (Details like eyelashes and belt buckles are not easy to include with drippy ink.) Putting more than one drawing on a page also makes children think a little bit about design and balance.

*Figure 37 - **Schematics**:* Blind Contour Drawing by a 7-year-old child. For this blind contour drawing, students were given a bowl of black ink and a variety of drawing tools, including thin and thick paintbrushes and twigs that were picked up in the yard. On the same piece of paper, they were asked to include two drawings, one using a thin twig and one using a thicker paintbrush. This kind of drawing exercise is a constructive and inventive way to approach artmaking because it keeps the emphasis on exploration (process) rather than on a prescribed end point (or product). Blind contours also give students a chance to play with thick and thin, draggy, and jumpy lines, odd shapes, and many other contrasting compositional elements.

A good way to approach drawing sessions is to have students pose for each other, sometimes wearing dress-up outfits like oversized hats or colorful shawls. Students can use diluted black tempera paint and a variety of drawing tools such as: twigs, pipe cleaners, chopsticks, old toothbrushes, cut-up sponges, or different kinds of paintbrushes. Other more conventional drawing materials such as pencils, markers, oil pastels, and dark crayons can also be used. Each time there is a new pose, the students can change drawing tools. Because it is uncomfortable for students to stand still, poses may not last more than a few minutes.

Certain kinds of projects, especially blind contours, generate a lot of laughter because students are trying to draw while not looking at their paper. This is clearly not easy to do, but it is a lot of fun to try. This method of drawing makes children feel good about their work because there is no way to make "mistakes." Drawings are naturally going to be exaggerated and distorted, but that is part of what makes them interesting.

Fabric-Painting Collage—You will need: fabric scraps, glue, water-based paint, inks, paintbrushes, canvas board, masonite, or heavy cardboard.

All that's needed are some discarded fabric materials, paint, glue, and a heavy board such as canvas board, cardboard, or masonite (bought at a lumber yard or a hardware store). The children can cut the fabric into any shapes they want and then collage it onto the board. White glue should be placed in a recycled plastic container and applied heavily to the back of the fabric using a paintbrush. The empty areas that have not been collaged can be painted with tempera, gouache, or printing inks. This project can result in some beautiful compositions, as one patterned, solid, or textured area randomly meets another.

Painting—You will need: water-based paints such as gouache, tempera, watercolors, water-based printing inks, paintbrushes, water-based crayons and paper.

The following painting projects work well with students this age and older:

1. *Self-Portraits with Real or Imaginary Pets*—Children are asked to draw pictures of themselves with real or imaginary pets. The following questions might stimulate interesting ideas about the subject: "Did you ever have a pet? Did you always want one? If you could have any pet you want, what would it be? What is the strangest pet you've ever seen or heard about? Who has a dog, a snake, a mouse, a salamander, a hamster, or a cat? What do you like the most about your pet? What is the funniest thing your pet does? What is the most annoying? Can you describe what your pet looks like?" If a few children could bring in some of their small animals like rabbits, guinea pigs, gerbils, or ham-

sters on the same day, the class could pet them, feed them, and draw them directly from life. Also, class trips, with sketchbooks, to zoological museums, the zoo, or the circus can always stimulate ideas for art projects. Students of all ages should be encouraged to paint over the entire surface of their paper and not just on a small corner it.

2. *Fantasy Creatures*–When working with pretend creatures, like those that are part animal and part human, children are asked to think about imaginary beings that have never been seen before. A good source for stimulating ideas on this topic is a fine arts museum where children can see ancient sculptures of mythological beings such as the centaur or the sphinx. Posters can also be displayed or pictures from art history books can be photocopied, enlarged, and then hung up in the classroom. The pictures are meant to be used as a reference point for students to get ideas and generate discussions about fantasy creatures before taking off on their own original projects.

3. *Kings, Queens, Healers, Masks, and Magical Beings with Special Powers*–Museum visits to look at statues of gods and goddesses, African masks, and Egyptian mummies are a great way to stimulate paintings about these subjects. Also, descriptions of ancient cultures may encourage students to create their own version of magical beings, healers, saints, warriors, or rulers. Any one of these projects could start off with a painting and continue into three-dimensional media like clay or papier maché, especially the masks. If it is not possible for students to visit a museum in person, they can be shown photographs from books or visit Internet sites of museum artworks. (See Chapter 6 for more ideas on using the Internet to explore the visual arts.)

4. *Sequential Story Paintings*–These are structured narrative paintings, similar to comic strips. Students can be given paper that is divided into 6 geometric shapes. This format makes it easier for students to conceptualize events happening in different time blocks. An example of a sequential story painting might be "A day in my life, from morning to night." Each box could depict an important part of the student's day. Or, the student can make up a character and develop adventures for him. As a long-term project, the student, using the same geometric format, can be asked to make a series of adventure stories that could comprise a book.

5. *Imagine Paintings*–These are paintings based on any idea or unfinished story that starts with the word "imagine." An example would be the following dream-like scenario: "Imagine that you were

walking home from school and you suddenly saw a pink house shaped like a spaceship. It had purple dots all over it and a bright yellow light was blinking on and off from a big open window. You got up close to it and looked inside. What did you see?" The student takes off from the story idea and visually completes it.

6. *Futuristic Projection Paintings*–These paintings relate to events that could happen in the future. A project idea for the student might be: "Picture yourself in 50 years as the powerful mayor of a big city. Draw yourself standing in the middle of the city that you govern. What are some of the differences between the way the world would look in the future and the way it looks now?"

7. *Dream Paintings*–Students are given a sheet of paper that is geometrically divided into 3 sections. One box should be bigger than the others, while the two smaller boxes should be the same size. In one small box, the students are asked:

1. to paint themselves before they go to bed. (They could be brushing their teeth, reading a book, or just doing whatever they do before bed.) In the other small box, they are asked:

2. to paint themselves sleeping.

In the larger box, they are asked:

3. to paint a memory of a vivid dream that they once had. If they can't remember a dream, they can make one up or just add pretend images onto a dream fragment that they do remember.

Mood Box Sculpture–You will need: a box, paper, dark colored felt-tip markers or tempera paint, paintbrushes, white glue or glue sticks, fishing line, and (optional) collage materials.

This project requires a strong, medium-sized packaging box with all four sides tightly closed. With paints and/or collage, children are asked to create a series of self-portraits showing how they look and feel when they are in a certain mood or have a particular feeling, like *happy, mad, sad, confused, hurt, surprised, or scared.* Children can associate specific facial expressions with different moods or feelings or they can paint moods abstractly. All paintings are done on paper and pasted with white glue or glue sticks onto all sides of the box. Paintings can also be photocopied so that some of the images can be repeated when they are pasted on the box. After the sculptures are done, they can be hung from the ceiling using fishing line. Put two staples into the top of the box, threading the fishing line underneath it. Then tie the line twice and staple it again, leaving a long piece to use for hanging (see Figure 38).

*Figure 38 - **Schematics**:* Mood Box Sculpture by a 7-year-old child. Mood box sculptures are not only fun to make, they also represent a good way for children to acknowledge their own moods and feelings. Displaying the sculpture is also a way of saying that emotional expression is important.

Clay (molding)—You will need: self-hardening clay, a plastic cover for the table, newspapers or a piece of canvas to put on top of the plastic, a dish of water, a spray bottle filled with water, inexpensive carving tools (or use Popsicle sticks or an old spoon), diluted white glue, paint, paintbrushes, collage materials, and small pieces of cardboard or newspaper to put under the sculpture while it's drying.

From this age on, most students are ready to mold clay into recognizable forms. If they start out the session by declaring, "I am going to make a giraffe today," encourage them to play around with the clay first before deciding exactly what to do next. Working from a large mass, they can mold the clay into masks, animals, machines, rocket ships, pretend creatures, or anything else they want to. They can squeeze the clay, pinch it, roll it, poke it, and push it around. A large lump of clay can be broken into several small parts. These smaller parts can then be attached together to make a new form.

Just as with *Preschematics* or any other age group, children's sculptures can be stored by covering them tightly with plastic wrap. If dry, they can be misted with water. While children are busy creating their sculptures, be sure to remind them to look at their work from all angles. Carving tools made of plastic, wood, and wire can be very helpful to the child as he tries to model the clay. If these tools cannot be found in a stationery or art store, use either end of an old spoon, a Popsicle stick, or the back end of a paintbrush to gouge out important areas. Textured designs can be drawn into the clay using a carving tool, a pencil, or a ballpoint pen. Decorative materials such as feathers, twigs, and pipe cleaners can be stuck into the sculpture before it dries.

Cracking clay (a problem for any age group) can sometimes be avoided by keeping the sculpture no more than $1/2$" thick all around. But, imposing this kind of limitation on children is not a good idea. They might become so concerned about the thickness or thinness of their sculpture that they may forget about what they were making in the first place. Particularly with this age group, the last thing we want to do is make children overly self-conscious or worried about getting their work "exact" or making it "right." (See the previous section under *Preschematics* for more information on drying procedures and various ways to prevent cracking.) When the sculpture is finished and has thoroughly dried, brush diluted white glue over the entire piece. The sculpture can be painted and collaged (optional) after the glue mixture dries.

String Prints–You will need: a piece of cardboard, a roll of string (twine), scissors, water-based printing ink, printing or drawing paper, a brayer (a small roller) and a piece of plexiglass covered with tinfoil for a palette.

String prints can be made using the following steps:

1. The first step involves getting a small, 8"x11" piece of cardboard, sold as "chip board" at stationery stores. The cardboard, or any surface that is used as a template to print from, is called a plate.

2. Squeeze glue on the board in a few places. Cut out pieces of twine and lay them in various shapes on top of the glued surface. The board has to dry thoroughly before it can be used for printing.

3. Print.

Instructions for Printing: The following 3 steps are applicable for string prints and also glue, linoleum, collage, and Styrofoam prints. Look in the next section (*Dawning Realists*) for instructions on printing monotypes.

1. *To Begin Printing:* After images have been created on the linoleum, Styrofoam, or cardboard, roll ink onto the surface with a brayer.

2. *To Transfer the Image:* To transfer the image from the plate to the paper, wet a piece of drawing or printing paper under the faucet and place it between two pieces of felt, cardboard, or paper towels. Rub gently to get off excess water. Take the damp paper and place it on top of the inked plate. Holding the paper steady, rub the back of the paper with the tips of your fingers. Then roll a dry brayer on top of the paper for a minute or two. Printing paper is preferred but all-purpose drawing paper can also be used. If you have a printing press, or access to one, use that if you can. Whichever method you use (hand rubbing, rolling with a dry brayer, or pressure from the printing press), the image will be transferred from the plate to the paper (see Figure 39).

3. *After the Image Has Been Printed:* For all printing projects, let the fin-

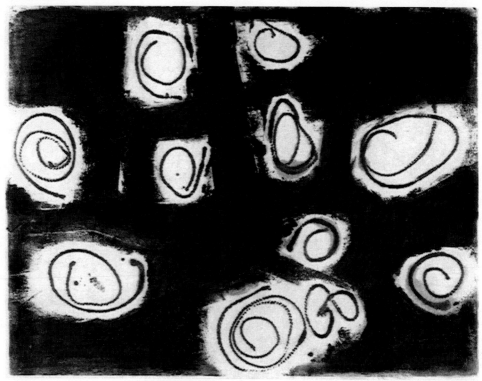

*Figure 39 - **Schematics**:* String Print by an 8-year-old child. This string print was made by gluing small pieces of string (made into circle shapes) onto a piece of cardboard, rolling ink over the surface, and then printing. Because it is hard to make anything too detailed out of the string, the tendency in this project is to make a few similar shapes and arrange them on the plate. Repetition of shapes is a good lesson in itself because it is an important rhythmic compositional tool that can be used effectively in future art projects.

ished print dry, then, as suggested for flat collage work, put the paper under a piece of plexiglass, with weights on top of it, for a few hours or overnight to prevent buckling.

Glue Prints—You will need: a piece of cardboard, white glue, a brayer, printing inks, paper, and a piece of plexiglass covered with tinfoil for a palette.

Glue prints can be made using the following steps:
1. Get a small 8"x11" piece of cardboard.
2. Squeeze glue onto the board in various shapes, like globs, dots,

circles, lines, shapes of people, buildings, animals, or whatever the student wants to make.

3. Let the plate dry overnight.

4. Print (see the previous section, *Instructions for Printing,* under "String Prints").

Styrofoam Prints—You will need: pieces of Styrofoam, a pencil, printing inks, and a roller.

Styrofoam prints can be made using the following steps:

1. Get pieces of Styrofoam from art stores or order some from an art supply catalogue.

2. With a sharp pencil, draw your image.

3. Print (see *Instructions for Printing,* under "String Prints"). Multiple prints can be made by simply cleaning off the Styrofoam plate under the sink, drying it, applying more ink and printing again.

Papier Maché (Standing) Sculpture—You will need: a wooden base, one toilet paper roll or ¹/₂ of a paper towel roll, masking tape or clear packaging tape, scissors, thin armature wire, newspapers or newsprint, white glue, paint and (optional) collage elements.

The following steps describe one way of making a standing papier maché sculpture:

1. Find or cut a wooden base, approximately 5" x 5".

2. Cut a paper towel roll in half or use a toilet paper roll and place it in the middle of the wooden base.

3. Tape the roll to the wooden base using masking tape or, even better, clear packaging tape.

4. Using sharp scissors, poke holes in the paper towel roll to attach sculpture wire through it. *Note:* Because the ends of the wire can be sharp, adults should make a loop out of them and then twist the wire before letting students use it.

5. Twist and bend the wire into any shape you wish to help create a structure (or armature) for the sculpture. Students can use masking tape to hold the shapes together and keep new ones from falling off.

6. Cover the structure with papier maché. Use a paintbrush to apply the glue-soaked strips of paper to the entire piece. Students, especially younger ones, will need help to insure that the wet and sticky paper is

wrapped tightly around their sculpture. When the piece dries, it can be painted and collage elements can be added to its surface.

Outdoor Outings—You will need: a clip board (a piece of cardboard and a clip), all-purpose drawing paper, and a pencil case filled with drawing materials such as dark pencils, china markers, and water-based crayons.

Outdoor outings can include trips to local libraries, sculpture gardens, fine arts and science museums, zoological museums, aquariums, private gardens, art galleries, dance studios, public parks, outdoor cafes, and anywhere else that students can become observers. Students can clip their paper and pencil cases to the drawing board. The rough drawings can be saved and used for project ideas in the future or they can be finished during another session.

Other Projects to Try: from Preschematics—Vegetable/Found Object Prints, Clay, Mixed Paper Collage, Crayon/Watercolor Resist, Papier Maché Puppets, and Found Object Box Sculptures (see Figure 40).

*Figure 40 - **Schematics:*** Found Object Box Sculpture by an 8-year-old child. This sculpture was made using a small box and pushing up the top to make a roof. The chimney was made from a piece of cardboard taped to the top of the roof. After the box was glued to the wooden base, the whole thing was covered with papier maché and painted. The student added play people later.

Other Suggestions: Museums may offer creative art programs for younger children on the weekends, after school, and during school vacations. Look into after-school activities at local public schools and private art classes for children that might be taught by experienced artists. Also, summer day camps may offer special programs in the visual arts.

Art References for the Younger Child—

Artists of interest might include:
19th century: Mary Cassatt (1844-1926), Paul Cézanne (1839-1906), Sarah Miriam Peale (1800-1885), Vincent van Gogh (1853-1890).

Early-mid 20th century: Alexander Calder (1898-1976. Children will especially enjoy looking at his mobiles, the *Circus,* and toys made out of boxes and tin cans), Marc Chagall (1887-1985), Joseph Cornell (1903-1973), Jean Dubuffet (1901-1985), William H. Johnson (1901-1970), Paul Klee (1879-1940), Gabriele Münter (1877-1962), Louise Nevelson (1899-1988), Georgia O'Keeffe (1887-1986).

Mid-late 20th century: Alice Aycock (b.1946), Romare Bearden (1911-1988), Helen Frankenthaler (b.1928), Carmen Lomas Garza (b.1948), Lois Mailou Jones (b.1905), Marisol (b.1930), Elizabeth Murray (b.1940), Claes Oldenburg (b.1929), Faith Ringgold (b.1930), Betye Saar (b.1926), George Segal (b.1924), Sandy Skoglund (b.1946), Andy Warhol (1928-1987).

Dawning Realists (9-12 Years Old)

Drawing—You will need: paper and one or more of the following— black tempera paint and paintbrushes or twigs, black felt-tip markers, china markers, conté crayons, oil pastels, charcoal pencils, or charcoal sticks.

Automatic Drawings, Contours, Blind Contours (see Figure 41), Cut Out Contour Collage, Imaginary Drawings, *Gesture Drawings* (quick drawings that capture the action or position of the figure), *Observational Drawings* (drawings that use direct observation as a starting point for a range of visual interpretations), and *Memory Drawings* (drawings that depend on the memory of something rather than on direct observation). Students enjoy gesture drawings because not only are they challenging to create, they are also fun to pose for. The person posing freezes in one position for about a minute, then takes another position, and so on. Students can pose for a series of drawings in 10-minute shifts. Memory drawings can involve putting objects on a table and having students study them for about 5 minutes. Then the objects can be taken away and students are asked to draw what they remember.

*Figure 41 - **Dawning Realists**:* Blind Contour Drawing by a 12-year-old child. This blind contour drawing was done quickly, using a paintbrush and diluted black paint. The student made an effort to concentrate on looking at the model and not at her paper. Students posed for one another, sometimes putting on hats, glasses, shawls, and other accessories to add more interest to the composition.

Linoleum Prints—You will need: a sheet of linoleum, a linoleum cutter (available at art stores or stationery stores), a brayer, water-based printing inks, and paper.

Note: This project needs a lot of supervision because the cutting tools are very sharp. I have found two solutions to the problem:

First, the student draws an image on the linoleum and then the adult cuts it out. Another option requires close supervision. You may allow only a few students at a time to work on a large table, but only under the following conditions:

1. Use a 3" clamp from the hardware store to affix the linoleum sheet to the table.

2. Students must have one arm in back of them while they use the other hand to cut, making strokes away from them. If the tool slips, it will move toward an empty place.

Linoleum prints can be made using the following steps:
1. Use a thin piece of linoleum.
2. Cut an image into it with a linoleum cutter.
3. Print (see the previous section, *Instructions for Printing*, under "String Prints" for directions). Multiple prints can be made by simply cleaning off the plate with water, drying it, applying more ink and printing again.

Collage Prints—You will need: a piece of cardboard or plexiglass to use as a plate, manila envelopes, index cards, cardboard scraps (no thicker than $^1/_4$"), Styrofoam scraps, textured fabric scraps, scissors, white glue, a brayer, printing inks, and paper.

The following steps describe one way of making collage prints:
1. Use a sturdy surface, such as plexiglass or cardboard for a plate.
2. Gather together scraps from pieces of Styrofoam, textured fabric materials such as lace or burlap, corregated cardboard, or manila envelopes that are ripped or cut into shapes.
3. Paste the shapes onto the plate. If you are using Styrofoam scraps, you can draw directly on them before or after you paste them to the plate. Apply white glue not only to the back of the shapes but also in slightly diluted amounts, to the front of the plate.
4. Let the plate dry thoroughly.
5. Print (see the previous section, *Instructions for Printing*, under "String Prints" for directions). Multiple prints can be made by cleaning off the plate, drying it, reapplying ink, and printing again (see Figure 42).

Figure 42 - ***Dawning Realists***: Collage Print by a 10-year-old child. This collage self-portrait print was made using Styrofoam shapes that were pasted to a cardboard plate. A few more scraps of string and other materials were added to the plate's surface before it was printed.

Monotype—You will need: a piece of plexiglass to use as a plate (a thin piece of wood or metal can also be used), a scrap piece of plexiglass (covered with tinfoil) for a palette, scrap materials, a brayer, water-based printing inks, watercolors, printing paper, some rags, and lots of paper towels. Monotypes can be hand printed or a printing press can be used.

A *monotype* is a one-of-a-kind (*mono*) print. Because this medium offers so much flexibility, there is no "standard" way to make a monotype. The following steps describe only one of the basic ways of making a monotype:

1. *Use a plate:* Buy a piece of plexiglass (preferable) about 10" x 12" from an art store or a hardware store. Plexiglass and other materials such as wood can be cut to your specifications.

2. *Roll the ink:* Using a brayer, roll printing ink onto the plate.

3. *Create an image:* Images can be made in the following ways: (a) *Taking away*—"Taking away" simply means removing some of the ink from the surface. This involves creating an image on the surface of the plate by rubbing with a rag, an old toothbrush, a finger, a rolled-up paper towel, a cut-up sponge, or whatever else you want to use, or scratching into the inked surface with a stick or a small piece of cardboard or any other blunt tool. (b) *Adding*—Rather than drawing into the surface, the term "adding" means that you introduce scraps and other materials to the plate. For example, small pieces of wire mesh, burlap, cut-up or ripped-up pieces of paper, found objects (no thicker than ¼"), and scraps of corrugated cardboard or textured fabric can be carefully placed on top of the inked-up plate. The scraps can be painted, in whatever colors you want, before you put them on the plate. If they are not painted, the shapes will come out white. Just before printing, ink can be randomly dropped on the scraps. The paint will splatter during the printing process, resulting in some very unpredictable and interesting effects.

4. *Print:* Because water-based printing inks dry fast, printing with these inks will have to be done quickly. Once the plate is finished, take a piece of printing paper and run it under the faucet to get it wet. Then place it between 2 pieces of felt or paper towels and remove the excess water. Place the damp paper on top of the plate and print either by hand, rubbing the back of the paper with a dry roller, or with a printing press. The image will be transferred from the plate to the paper. If the image is too light and needs more work, you can paint directly on it immediately after you finish printing. Other kinds of art materials besides paint, such as oil pastels, collage scraps, and charcoal pencils can also be used to complete the image (see Figure 43).

*Figure 43 - **Dawning Realists**:* Monotype by an 11-year-old child. The first step in making this monotype was applying black water-based ink to a piece of plexiglass with a roller. Then the student made shapes out of paper and cardboard and also used some precut scraps. Most of the shapes were painted (but some were left blank) before they were carefully placed on top of the inked surface to be printed.

Some other ways to make monotypes:

1. Watercolor Monotype without Printing Inks – You will need:
a plexiglass plate, watercolor tube paints, water-based crayons, a palette, paper (printing paper works best) and paintbrushes.

Without using a roller, you can draw and paint directly on the plate with water-soluble crayons and watercolor tube paints. Make the lines as dark as you can. In this process, the plate does not have to be printed right away because wet paper will pick up the dried watercolor any time. When you are ready, place a piece of very damp printing paper on top of the plate and print, either by hand or with a press. If the print comes out too lightly, you can use other art materials like water-based crayons, gouache, oil pastels, watercolor tube paints, dark and light drawing pencils, china markers, and charcoal pencils to enhance the image. Collage scraps can also be added. But, no matter how the monotype is approached, it is a process-oriented and fluid medium that invites play and manipulation. Rather than being seen as a final product after one try, the print can be thought of as a sketch or a work in progress.

2. Water-based Monotype with Printing Inks—You will need: a plexiglass plate, water-based printing inks, paintbrushes, and paper (printing paper works best).

Without using a roller, you can paint directly on the plexiglass, with printing inks and paintbrushes. (Think of the plexiglass as a canvas.) But remember that any time water-based printing inks are used, the plate should be printed immediately because the paints dry fast. Put a damp piece of paper on the plate and print. After the image is transferred, you can continue painting on the paper and expanding the image in any way that meets your artistic vision.

String-Print Box Sculpture—You will need: string prints, a cardboard box, glue, and fishing line (bought at a hardware store) if you want to hang it.

(See the previous section, under *Schematics*, for instructions on how to make string prints.) Make a series of about 10 string prints. Since the cardboard plates can be reprinted, you can repeat the same print, with the same color, a few times. If you want to change the color, rinse the plate in the sink and let it dry before applying a different color paint for printing. Use a sturdy cardboard box with all four sides closed. Once all the string prints are dry, cut them to fit the box and collage them to every side. The box can then hang from the ceiling or be placed on a table (see Figure 44).

*Figure 44 - **Dawning Realists:*** String-Print Box Sculpture by a 10-year-old child. In order to construct this project, first the student needed to make a series of many string prints. After the prints were made, they were pasted (with no space between them) on all sides of a box.

Painting—You will need: water-based paints such as gouache, watercolors, printing inks, water-based crayons, paper, paintbrushes, collage materials, and glue.

In addition to all of the painting projects for *Schematics*, the following projects also work well for students this age and older:

1. *Life-Cycle Paintings*–These are narrative paintings that deal with the past, present, and future. In order to get this project going, first, using a ruler, divide the paper into six or eight symmetrical shapes. They can be squares, rectangles, triangles, or whatever works evenly on the page. The older child is essentially drawing himself in different stages of his life. Inside the geometrical shapes, the student paints images of babyhood, nursery school, primary school, high school, adulthood, and finally, old age. This project may be particularly meaningful for the older child, especially as he matures into adulthood, and becomes more self-reflective (see Figure 45).

*Figure 45 - **Dawning Realists**:* Life-Cycle Painting by a 12-year-old preteen. Creating a life-cycle painting meant that the preteen had to think about different stages of his life including his early childhood and his life in the future. From the upper left corner (clockwise) to the bottom left corner, the student used a generic schema to represent himself from babyhood to old age. Notice that throughout the more adult stages in his life, he sees himself as being connected to books and music.

2. *Patterned and Textural Paintings*—Students can be given paper that is divided into 6 squares. In each square they can create their own version of patterns or designs that relate to (a) nature and/or (b) urban environments. To create interest in this project, it would be a good idea for the teacher to show slides that reflect patterns in nature such as human or plant cells, snowflakes, vegetable forms, grains of wood, ice formations, leaves, stones, twigs, textures of tree bark, or tree rings. Also stimulating to look at are photos or slides of the textures and designs of living creatures such as starfish, chameleons, peacocks, turtles, armadillos, and zebras. For urban environments, students can look at photos or slides of repeated design elements in ripped-up billboards, subway grates, piled-up garbage cans, street architecture, and graffiti.

3. *Ancient Past/Present Paintings*—Artifacts from lost civilizations such as dinosaur fossils and cave paintings can be looked at, either through slides, books, or on the Internet to get ideas for paintings that connect some aspect of antiquity with the present.

4. *Perfect World Paintings*—Discussions about environmental concerns and social problems such as racial, economic, gender, and class inequality, powerlessness, and violence could generate paintings depicting a more socially equal, gentle, peaceful, and idealized world.

5. *Invention Paintings*—Students can picture themselves as brilliant, magical, and world-famous inventors. The suggestion is: "Draw yourself standing next to 5 prize-winning inventions that you created in order to make the world a better place."

Hanging Papier Maché Sculpture—You will need: wire, papier maché, paint, paintbrushes, fishing line, and collage materials.

Papier maché is a flexible medium that not only suits young children, but all ages. (See projects in previous sections.) Hanging sculptures are constructed in a similar way to that of the standing sculpture, (as described in *Schematics*), except, in this one, there is no wooden base involved. The following steps describe one way of making a hanging sculpture:

1. Get armature wire and mold it into a shape. You can make an animal shape, a fish, a person, a snake, a star, a circle, a triangle, a square, or any other amorphous or geometric shape.

2. Stuff newspapers inside the shape.

3. Wrap more wire or masking tape, or both, around the structure to keep the newspapers tightly inside the shape.

4. Using a paintbrush, cover the shape with strips of sticky papier maché.

5. As the papier maché strips are being wrapped around the armature, put a paper clip (with a piece of it sticking out) on top of the sculpture so that it can be used later as a hook.

6. After the sculpture dries, it can be painted, collaged, and hung from the ceiling with transparent fishing line. Also, strips of colorful fabric material and/or other kinds of scraps can be stapled to the sculpture to hang down from it or stick out from it.

Self-Portrait/Memory Box Sculpture—You will need: a recycled or self-made box, collage elements, such as magazine scraps, personal items, and objects that can be pasted in addition to glue, paint, and paint-brushes.

This sculpture involves having the older child create a self-portrait for the outside of the box. On the inside, she recreates (through collage and/or paint) events, moments, or impressions of places or objects that evoke emotional memory for her. Emotional memory implies more than just the act of objectively remembering something. It means that a particular object, place, event, or moment in time brings up strong feelings. Through painting and collage, students can recreate these moments of special significance. Each student also can bring in important items for her box, such as collected coins, old report cards, a menu from a favorite restaurant, a note from a best friend, a small piece from a broken toy, fabric scraps from old clothes, photocopies of family photographs or pictures from pop culture magazines, ticket stubs (to sports events, music concerts, dramatic performances, dance recitals, movies), baseball cards, playbills, wrappers from a favorite candy bar or snacks, ripped-up parts of an old diary, discarded letters, or even real pieces of an old baby blanket. Items must be small enough and light enough to be pasted inside the box without weighing it down too much. Slides of the work of artists such as Joseph Cornell and Betye Saar, who infuse humble objects with poetic meaning, can be shown and discussed.

Plasticine—You will need: plasticine, and possibly a carving tool.

Plasticine (also called *plastina*) is an oily and sometimes colored modelling clay that cannot be baked and never totally hardens. The more it is handled, the more pliable it becomes. It is usually sold in stationery and art stores and it often comes in small packages. Children can mold it easily and then let it stay that way indefinitely. But they can also return to the sculpture at a later date, rework it, and turn it into something else.

Blind Contour Creatures—You will need: black ink, paintbrushes, water-based paints, collage, glue, and paper.

Students are given a piece of paper that has been divided into four squares. Taking turns modelling, students are asked to create four blind contour figure drawings. After they have completed all four boxes, most drawings will look like inky blobs, or just amorphous shapes. Students are then asked to turn their shapes into imaginary creatures, using water-based paints and collage. Because blind contour drawings result in such fluid and abstract works, this is a great exercise for students this age. It reflects the notion that artwork can evolve from one stage to another and that art is more about creative decision-making than it is about "correct" ways to draw or paint something.

Other Projects to Try: from Preschematics—Vegetable/Found Object Prints, Clay, Mixed Paper Collage, Papier Maché Puppets, Found Object Box Sculptures (see Figure 46); from Schematics—Fabric-Painting Collage (any or all) Painting Projects, Mood Box Sculptures, Clay, String Prints, Glue Prints, Styrofoam Prints, Papier Maché Standing Sculptures, Outdoor Drawing Excursions.

*Figure 46 - **Dawning Realists:** Found Object Box Sculpture by an 11-year-old child. This project involved putting together a few boxes (bought in a stationery store) and some pieces of cardboard. The boxes and cardboard scraps were attached together with masking tape and then pasted to a wooden board. Once the boxes were put together, the student decided that the construction looked like a house or an apartment. She made a chimney by cutting off a piece of a paper towel roll and attaching it with tape to the top of the sculpture. Then the entire sculpture was covered with papier mâché and painted. Later, the student added play furniture to one of the rooms of the house. Windows and doors were made out of paper, magic markers, and paint. The flowers and leaves around the house came from cut-out scraps of fabric material.

Other Suggestions: Art workshops may be found for older children in community centers, museums, art schools, public school programs, summer camps, and private studio settings. Class choices for older children might include: drawing, beginning photography, ceramics, sculpture, painting, printing, computer workshops, and papermaking.

Art References for the Older Child–Art movements to explore: Expressionism, Impressionism, Pop Art, and Surrealism. Artists of interest might include:

16th-17th century: El Greco (1541-1614), Judith Leyster (1609-1660), Caterina van Hemessen (1527-1566), Jan Vermeer (1632-1675).

18th century: François Boucher (1703-1770), Jacques-Louis David (1748-1825), Angelica Kauffmann (1741-1807), Marie-Louise-Elisabeth Vigée-Lebrun (1755-1842).

19th century: Mary Cassatt (1844-1926), Paul Cézanne (1839-1906), Paula Modersohn-Becker (1876-1907), Sarah Miriam Peale (1800-1885), Lilly Martin Spencer (1822-1902), Vincent van Gogh (1853-1890).

Early-mid 20th century: Alexander Calder (1898-1976), Joseph Cornell (1903-1973), Salvador Dalí (1904-1989), Sonia Terk Delaunay (1885-1979), Jean Dubuffet (1901-1985), Max Ernst (1891-1976), Hannah Höch (1889-1978), Edward Hopper (1882-1967), William H. Johnson (1901-1970), Frida Kahlo (1910-1954), Wassily Kandinsky (1866-1944), Käthe Kollwitz (1867-1945), Lee Krasner (1908-1984), Henri Matisse (1869-1954), Joan Miró (1893-1983), Piet Mondrian (1872-1944), Gabriele Münter (1877-1962), Alice Neel (1900-1984), Louise Nevelson (1899-1988), Georgia O'Keeffe (1887-1986), Pablo Picasso (1881-1973), Jackson Pollock (1912-1956).

Mid-late 20th century: Alice Aycock (b.1946), Jean-Michel Basquiat (1960-1988), Romare Bearden (1911-1988), Mary Frank (b.1933), Helen Frankenthaler (b.1928), Carmen Lomas Garza (b.1948), Duane Hanson (1925-1996), Keith Haring (1958-1990), Jasper Johns (b.1930), Lois Mailou Jones (b.1905), Roy Lichtenstein (b.1923), Marisol (b.1930), Elizabeth Murray (b.1940), Claes Oldenburg (b.1929), Bridget Riley (b.1931), Faith Ringgold (b.1930), Alison Saar (b.1956), Betye Saar (b.1926), Raymond Saunders (b.1934), George Segal (b.1924), Sandy Skoglund (b.1946), Nancy Spero (b.1926), Andy Warhol (1928-1987).

Chapter 6

ART PROJECTS FOR ADOLESCENTS
AGES 12 TO 17

WORKING TOGETHER: THE PARENT/TEACHER ROLE

Developmentally, teenagers are going through an intense period of discovery where they are continually reinventing themselves. They are also accomodating to new cultural and social influences at a very fast rate. Regardless of what they are involved in, adolescents are likely to have a unique and interesting perspective on the world. They may also express passion about their beliefs. Their ideas, interests, and experiences are very important to them and they should be taken seriously. Although adolescents may act like they don't need support from adults, just the opposite is true. Teenagers are forever seeking approval not only from their peers, but on a certain level, from parents and teachers, too. Adults should pay close attention to teenage emotional and psychological needs, because some adolescents may need more support at this stage in life than they did when they were younger.

Art can be very therapeutic for teens because it provides a vehicle to deal with issues that, in some cases, cannot be talked about. But teenagers may have a harder time exploring personal issues through art if they feel intimidated about their work or if they feel that they have to "explain" themselves to people who don't understand or support what they are doing. The process of working creatively with teenagers requires open-ended collaboration and mutual respect. It involves giving teens their own space, but also being available to support them and give them help when needed. Parents can contribute by setting up an environment where artmaking can happen, informally, spontaneously, and naturally. But after that, they should leave teenagers alone while they are working. For this age group, artmaking is essentially a quiet, solitary, and meditative activity. Teens (like the rest of us) need space to explore their own creative process where people are not looking over their shoulder (see Chapter 4, under "Creativity Killers," for other ways not to smother creativity).

The Internet can also provide teens with an exciting new way to discover the visual arts. The following is only a partial list of the art topics and art experiences that can be explored on the Internet: public and private school art curricula, museum and gallery exhibits (national and international), contemporary and historical art movements, art history resources, biographical information about contemporary or historical artists, indigenous artworks from different cultures, art books, community education courses such as art appreciation classes, art terminology, information about applying to art schools and art programs in universities, as well as artwork from children and adult artists around the world.

There are also on-line "bulletin boards" that provide opportunities for students to post messages about art-related topics. Teens can scan color photos of their artwork into the computer and they can even become involved with on-line art discussion groups. As parents and teachers, we should be familiar with some of this art material so that we can talk to our teens about the information they have acquired.

To connect with adolescents, not only should we be aware of what is on the Internet, but also what is being reflected in the pop culture scene (contemporary music, movies, and TV shows). Cultural trends, prevailing attitudes, and broader social problems can be discussed in class and then certain aspects of these issues could be used as themes for artmaking.

In art class, the teacher should present art projects that are structured but creative, allowing for interesting and unpredictable results. It is also important for the studio environment to be relaxed and open, and for students to feel accepted for who they are. The art room should be a sanctuary where ideas can be thrown around, music can be played, and discussions can be generated about topics that are important in students' lives. Examples of topics that might come out of conversations in class, and could later be turned into themes for art projects, are: changing identity, transformation, power and powerlessness, loneliness, leaving home, adventures, self-esteem, social acceptance, friendships, romantic love, good against evil, competition, and alienation. The main role for parents and teachers at this stage is to help facilitate adolescent artwork through mutual problem-solving, stimulation, and support.

Individual Needs, Feedback, and the Creative Process

Many teens have stopped seeing themselves as creative or "skilled" in art, either because of intimidating and/or ill-prepared teachers or lack of support somewhere along the line. When dealing with adolescents, we need to be as flexible with them as we are with young children, if not even more so. If the art projects we suggest are not working for the student, we need to modify them or consider changing the projects completely. Projects that work the best for students who might be just starting to make art again are those for which the possibility of "right" or "wrong" results do not apply. Examples could be: collages, blind contour drawings, monotypes, glue or string prints.

In working with teenagers, as with any other age group, it is important to consider the way we relate to the artwork *after* it is completed. The teen may be ultra-sensitive to criticism about her artwork because it has personal and symbolic meaning for her and she strongly identifies with it. Sharing artwork with others, especially at this age, can be a little bit like allowing a stranger to read your diary. Adults should wholeheartedly support teens for their creative efforts. But sometimes we *think* we are being supportive to teens, when, in fact, we're not. For example, parents and teachers frequently (and innocently) make remarks to adolescents that inadvertantly make them feel insecure about their artwork and their art ability in general. In looking at student drawings of the figure, I have often heard adults ask teenagers questions like, "What happened to the hands?" or "Is that where the head should be?" or "Aren't the arms too long?" These types of questions assume that the goal behind the student's artwork is to make it look "real." Instead, the opposite may be true. The adolescent may be trying to make a personal statement that has nothing to do with naturalism (the attempt to represent subject matter objectively). Instead, she may be attempting to break new ground by expressing a mood, an idea, or a feeling through exaggeration and distortion. A better approach would be, as with young children, first to give adolescents some positive feedback, and then to ask them to discuss their process of creating.

It is important to remember that adolescents are still involved in searching for an independent sense of self. Adolescent artwork can sometimes be seen as a window into this difficult process. Often, the teenager who is sharing her art with us is also expressing (and exposing) some of her innermost thoughts and feelings. As discussed in Chapter 4 under "Working with Adolescent Artists," teenage artwork may allow us temporary entrance into their private world, but we are not entirely welcome there (and we shouldn't be). After taking the risk of showing us her work, the last thing the teen wants to deal with is single-minded adults who dismiss or disparage her efforts.

Planning and Brainstorming

Although art projects should be carefully planned, sometimes we need to switch gears unexpectedly. If the project that we spend the most time planning (and the one that seems the most exciting) turns out, inexplicably, to be a dud, we need to brainstorm our way out of a potentially boring, unproductive, or even chaotic art session. Thinking creatively and being able to change easily from one project to another is a crucial way to save a session and turn it into one that is interesting and challenging. It is important to have the right kinds of art materials around to be able to do just that.

When a project isn't working for an adolescent, she will usually tell us bluntly that she is bored or she doesn't know what to do. If her project has turned into a dead end, we can suggest that she put it away and start something else. She may want to work on some other projects instead. Sometimes working on more than one project at a time is a good idea. But, if the student insists on sticking with the original project and cannot let it go, we can help her figure out how to change it. If our initial ideas fail to interest her, we could try a more adventurous and even a more radical suggestion. For example, the student could "destroy" and reconstruct the project by ripping or cutting up the work and collaging it into something new and unrecognizable. She may be shocked by the suggestion or she may just be turned off by it. On the other hand, it may expand the way she thinks about art.

Pseudo-Naturalists (12-14 Years Old)

Drawing—You will need: paper and one or more of the following— 6B pencils, charcoal pencils or charcoal sticks, china markers, conté crayons, black tempera paint, paintbrushes, twigs, water-based crayons, black felt-tip markers, or oil pastels.

Automatic Drawings, Blind Contour Drawings, Gesture Drawings, Cut out Contour Collage, Imaginary Drawings, Memory Drawings, Observational Drawings (see Figure 47), *Moving Figure Drawings* (the model slowly moves as the student tries to draw some aspect of her movement), *Group Figure Drawings* (more than one model poses at the same time), *Modelled Drawings* (drawings that emphasize light and dark tones of the form, such as shadows and folds), *Opposite Hand Drawings* (if the student ordinarily draws with her right hand, she draws with her left hand instead), *Two-Handed Drawings* (drawing with two hands at the same time, sometimes with different materials in each hand) and *Conversation Drawings* (students pick a partner and they share the same

Figure 47 - Pseudo-Naturalists: Drawing by a 14-year-old teen. Using a photograph as a reference point, this work of art was made by a student who was involved in drawing historical buildings in her town. The drawing, called "Town Hall," was done with black ink without using pencil first. Notice the attention to detail and the sophisticated use of perspective.

piece of paper. One student makes a drawing and then gives it to a partner. The partner then draws on the paper. Drawing on the partner's paper means adding to her work or, at times, even drawing over her image. The communal drawing gets passed back and forth for a while, until both partners decide that the visual conversation is over).

20th Century Artifact Construction—You will need: some or all of the following—found objects, junk and paint for the sculpture, and a piece of masonite, cardboard or wood, colored paper, magazine scraps, photocopies of random images, fabric materials, paint, and glue for flat collage.

Students are asked to create a three-dimensional construction or a flat collage that could be viewed as a cultural artifact that reflects something about the times that we live in. Questions that students could think about while they are working on the piece might be: "What do these artifacts say about our society? What would people hundreds of years from now learn about the 20th century by looking at these artworks? What would people in the Middle Ages think of the way we live now?"

Examples of things students can use for the three-dimensional construction or flat collage are: newspaper clippings or photocopies from books; crushed-up soda cans; bottle tops; ripped-up scraps from wrapping paper; strings; old telephone pages; inserts from consumer products such as hair dyes, skin lotions, and other drug store items; computer printouts; advertising copy from magazines; torn-up fragments of food packaging items such as candy bar wrappers, cereal boxes, and other food boxes as well as lightweight broken pieces from toys or machine parts. Students can view slides of artists such as Robert Rauschenberg who created assembled constructions starting in the 1950s that dealt with political, social, and psychological aspects of the culture. His work combined painting with miscellaneous objects such as pillows, clocks, road signs, and other odd junk (he even turned his own bed into an art piece). Students can also look at pictures of Cubist collages by Pablo Picasso and Georges Braque that incorporate found materials such as wallpaper scraps, ticket stubs, music sheets, rope, and sand.

Note: After all collages are finished, they should be covered with a piece of plexiglass and a heavy board, for a few hours or overnight, to prevent warping.

Painting—You will need: paper, cardboard, canvas, wood, (or whatev-
er surface is available to paint on), water-based paint, paintbrushes,
any kind of palette, paper towels, a rag, and collage materials
(optional).

All the painting projects from *Schematics* and *Dawning Realists* are
relevant to this age as well as the following ones:

1. ***Newspaper Story Paintings***—A good way to stimulate ideas for
mixed-media painting projects is through newspaper stories. Students
can be encouraged to look at the newspaper every day in order to collect one story a week for use as an art project. The daily newspaper
can be kept in class and, if there is a photocopy machine available, students can duplicate the stories that they want to work with. If a student
only wants to collect comics, that's fine, too. Those stories or comics
could be used as impetus to create original artworks. Some topics that
are especially good for generating ideas might be environmental stories dealing with pollution or endangered species, stories about
teenagers who have gotten into the news either through good deeds or
by getting into trouble, and stories that have science fiction implica-
tions like those about extraterrestrial beings, sightings of UFOs, or
unexplained phenomenon like symmetrical circles appearing in wheat
fields. One student I worked with collected stories about domestic
abuse and used them in an emotionally moving and chilling mixed-
media painting. She photocopied the violent news articles and juxta-
posed parts of them with fragmented visual images of domesticity such
as flowered wallpaper and cookies coming out of the oven. The artwork was not only therapeutic for the student to create, but it also
raised social and political awareness about this critical issue.

2. ***Pop Music Poetry Paintings***—Students, taking turns in different art
sessions, can choose meaningful song or poetry fragments to share
with the class. The fragments can be written on the board or played
on a tape recorder. Presentations should take no longer than five minutes. The focus of the project is for the class to create a painting that
takes off from the specific literary narrative or musical phrase introduced by the student. Instrumental music such as jazz or classical can

be used as well as music that involves words such as blues, hip-hop, pop, or funk. The poetry can be taken from any source the student finds interesting (including his own imagination).

3. *Pop Star Paintings (or Posters)*—Pictures of pop stars can be brought in by the students and used as a reference for a painting. If students don't have pictures of anyone they like, they can make up their own versions of music stars. Another idea is to ask them to paint themselves as famous performers playing in front of thousands of people. Students can also design posters for real or imaginary music groups.

4. *Lost on an Island Paintings*—Students are given a large piece of paper and asked to make a dot on the middle of the top edge. Then they use a ruler to make a straight line from the dot to each of the bottom corners of the paper. There should be only two lines on the paper because the bottom of the paper makes up the bottom of a triangle. In each of the three sections, students are asked to paint the 3 things that they could not live without if they were lost on a desert island. Students are encouraged to use up all the space by filling in all areas with paint, collage, or other art materials.

5. *Pretend Family Paintings*—Students are asked to create a portrait of a pretend family eating dinner. They do not have to include themselves in the painting. The paintings can depict real people or imaginary beings. The pretend family might be from another country or possibly from another planet. Students can make bizarre creatures that are half human, half animal, or half insect. After the paintings are finished, if there is time, students can share their work with the class and describe each of the family members.

6. *Childhood Memory Paintings*—Teenagers are asked to bring in a photograph of themselves as young children. Using the photograph as a stimulus, they can create a painting connected to some aspect of childhood memory. Paintings could have a broad range of interpretation. They do not have to represent a linear narrative. An abstract, stream-of-consciousness, mixed-media approach can be used. All forms of visual expression are encouraged.

7. *Fly on the Wall Paintings*—Students are asked to pretend that they are a fly on the wall of someone else's house. The house could belong to a teacher, a movie star, a friend's family, a reclusive or strange neighbor, or anyone who seems mysterious or interesting. The idea is to create an imaginary scenario about someone else's life. If students cannot think of anyone specific, they can make up a character.

8. *Beauty/Ugly Collage Paintings*—Because standards of beauty are so variable, beauty (an issue very close to the heart of adolescents) can be explored from the perspective of cultural differences and historical periods. Photos can be shown of Victorian fashions once considered to be beautiful such as ostrich-feather hats, bustles, and petticoats for women and bowler hats, knee-breeches, and waistcoats for men. Students can also look at pictures of tribal societies that engage in scarring, piercing, cutting, painting, and decorating the face and body. It is also worth noting that, although we live in a society that idolizes slender bodies, historically, being thin was not always thought to be attractive or desirable. Discussions exploring variations of cultural aesthetic standards, the transitory nature of beauty, and the concept of inner beauty may stimulate student paintings on this theme.

Students can be given a piece of paper that is divided in half. On one side, they can collage or paint images of whatever they think is beautiful. On the other side, they can create what they think is unattractive or ugly. Images to be considered might be pop culture pictures; nature scenes including tornadoes, floods, and hurricanes, wild animals, exotic insects; hairstyles; fashion styles; cars; comic book characters; imaginary scenarios; pretend creatures (human and/or animal); and fantasy people.

9. *Doodle/Collage Paintings*—Since almost everyone doodles, students can be asked to collect their doodles and bring in a pile of them to class by a certain date. The doodles can then be photocopied in multiples and handed back to the students. The photocopies and/or originals can be collaged upside-down, backwards, on top of each other, or any way the student wants, using a heavy board as a surface to paste on. This collage should be viewed as a work in progress because more doodles can be added later. Images can be crossed out, painted over, or changed in any way the student desires while the piece is being put together.

10. *Painting Set-Ups*—Regardless of what projects are planned, interesting and varied still life environments should be set up in the art room. If students are not interested in the class project, they can still find something stimulating to work on. Painting set-ups can include any of the following: the figure or a few figures combined (with students posing for one another); objects such as old tables, chairs and stools; stacks of boxes; bicycles; junk objects like machine parts; face masks; wood scraps; plastic skeletons; bird cages (and live birds, if possible); and colorful, patterned bedspreads or wall hangings. Young adolescents enjoy working directly from observation and experimenting with a variety of media. Students can work on expressionistic aspects of painting or on naturalistic qualities such as proportion, shading, and perspective. It is important for students to know that there are many styles of artmaking and many choices about how to approach a subject.

Ripped-up Photocopy Collage—You will need: paper, black tempera paint or printing inks, paintbrushes, scissors, and glue.

Arrange for students to do a series of contour drawings of figures, using black paint on white paper. Students can model for each other. Choose one of their drawings and make four photocopies of it. After giving the students back their copied drawings, suggest that they cut or rip the drawings (deconstructing them) and collage them onto a heavy board. The idea is to make them into something that looks completely different from the original drawings. If possible, look at slides or photos of the deconstructed paintings or collages of Lee Krasner and Willem DeKooning. After the piece has been collaged, it can be worked on and changed even more, with pencils, crayons, or other media (see Figure 48).

*Figure 48 - **Pseudo-Naturalists***: Ripped-up Photocopy Collage by a 14-year-old teen. Photocopies of old drawings were cut up, reconfigured, and pasted to a heavy board to create this original collage. None of the old work is recognizable in the new piece.

Television Sculpture—You will need: a square-shaped wooden or cardboard box with one side opened, paint, collage materials, twigs, wire, a drill, paints, paintbrushes, collage materials, and glue.

The students can either build a wooden box (some of them may be taking carpentry classes at school) or they can use an old cardboard one. At any rate, the box will need to have some way to affix the TV antennae to the top of it. If you are working with a wooden box, you can drill two holes on top into which two twigs (representing the attennae) can be glued. Alternatively, a cardboard box can have two holes poked into its top with a sharp scissors. Then a heavy wire (twisted on the top so that no one gets poked) is attached to the box from the inside.

The student is then asked to portray television in a critical way. But, before students can even think about the effect that TV has had on their lives, they need to change their role from passive participant (TV watcher) to one of active observer (TV analyst). Some questions the student can ask herself as she is making her own visual statement about television are as follows: "How does TV make me feel? How has it influenced my life? What is good about it? What is bad about it?" Some themes that students can explore in this project are violence on TV, hyperactive visual images, unhealthy commercial messages, and mixed up body images, especially for girls (see Figure 49).

*Figure 49 - **Pseudo-Naturalists:** Television Sculpture by a 13-year-old teen. This project was made with the help of a carpenter who built the box out of wood. Two holes were drilled on top of the box for the antennae, which were made out of twigs. This student approached the TV project from the point of view of a young girl who is getting mixed messages from TV shows and advertisers about how she should look and what kinds of foods she should eat. On the inside of the box, she put a photograph of a tall, thin, "perfect" looking model next to a picture of a piece of gooey chocolate cake. In a statement about her sculpture she wrote: "I thought that an important message that TV was giving kids was that if you wanted to get anywhere in life, you had to look like a model. TV is very contradictory because it also tells us that in order to be popular we should eat fatty foods like cakes, hamburgers, and pizzas."*

Other Suggestions: Young teens might be able to take classes in ceramics (using hand-building and/or a potter's wheel), painting, drawing, sculpture, woodworking, computer graphics and/or animation, video, fiber art, printmaking, book-making, or mixed media through after school programs, museums, art schools, intensive art workshops, summer arts camps, or private studio settings.

Other Projects to Try: from Preschematics—Vegetable/Found Object Prints, Mixed Paper Collage, Crayon/Watercolor Resist; from Schematics—Painting Projects, Clay, Fabric-Painting Collage, Mood Box Sculptures, String Prints, Glue Prints, Papier Maché Standing Sculptures, Outdoor Drawing Excursions; from Dawning Realists— Painting Projects, Linoleum Prints, Monotypes (see Figure 50), Hanging Papier Maché Sculptures, String-Print Box Sculptures, Self-Portrait/Memory Boxes (see Figure 51), Plasticine, Collage Prints.

Figure 50 - Pseudo-Naturalists: Monotype by a 13-year-old teen. After applying black ink to a plexiglass plate with a roller, this student cut out shapes to be placed on top of the inked surface. Besides using water-based inks, she used tubes of watercolors which she dripped on top of the surface of some of the shapes to create interesting and unexpected results.

*Figure 51- **Pseudo-Naturalists**:* Self-Portrait/Memory Box by a 12-year-old preteen. This memory box was done using a photographic self-portrait (photocopied and used repeatedly on several sides of the sculpture), drawings, scraps of paper, found objects, and paint. On the inside of the box the student included a photograph of her parents, her siblings, and her cat. She also put in a discarded peanuts wrapper (one of her favorite snacks), a picture of a piano, and a drawing of herself surrounded by books and writing.

Art References for Young Adolescents–Art movements to explore: Abstract Expressionism, Cubism, Conceptual Art, Dada, Earth Art, Expressionism, Graffiti Art, Impressionism, Photorealism, Pop Art, Surrealism. Artists of interest might include:

16th-17th century: El Greco (1541-1614), Giovanna Garzoni (1600-1670), Judith Leyster (1609-1660), Jan Vermeer (1632-1675).
18th century: François Boucher (1703-1770), Angelica Kauffmann (1741-1807), Marie-Louise-Elisabeth Vigée-Lebrun (1755-1842).
19th century: Mary Cassatt (1844-1926), Paul Cézanne (1839-1906), Winslow Homer (1836-1910), Berthe Morisot (1841-1895), Vincent van Gogh (1853-1890).
Early-mid 20th century: Alexander Calder (1898-1976), Sonia Terk Delaunay (1885-1979), Marcel Duchamp (1887-1968), Alberto

Giacometti (1901-1966), Barbara Hepworth (1903-1975), Hannah Höch (1889-1978), Edward Hopper (1882-1967), William H. Johnson (1901-1970), Frida Kahlo (1910-1954), Käthe Kollwitz (1867-1945), René Magritte (1898-1967), Alice Neel (1900-1984), Louise Nevelson (1899-1988), Georgia O'Keeffe (1887-1986), Pablo Picasso (1881-1973), Jackson Pollock (1912-1956).

Mid-late 20th century: Alice Aycock (b.1946), Jean-Michel Basquiat (1960-1988), Romare Bearden (1911-1988), John Biggers (b.1924), Christo (b.1935) and Jeanne-Claude (b.1935), Chuck Close (b.1940), Audrey Flack (b.1931), Mary Frank (b.1933), Helen Frankenthaler (b.1928), Nancy Graves (1940-1995), Duane Hanson (1925-1996), Keith Haring (1958-1990), Lois Mailou Jones (b.1905), Roy Lichtenstein (b.1923), Marisol (b.1930), Ana Mendieta (1948-1985), Joan Mitchell (1926-1992), Elizabeth Murray (b.1940), Yoko Ono (b.1933), Howardena Pindell (b.1943), Rose Piper (b.1917), Robert Rauschenberg (b.1925), Faith Ringgold (b.1930), George Segal (b.1924), Andy Warhol (1928-1987).

Adolescent Art (14-17 years old)

Drawing—You will need: paper and one or more of the following— 6B pencils, charcoal pencils, black china markers, conté crayons, charcoal sticks, a kneaded eraser, black ink or tempera paint, and twigs or paintbrushes, water-based crayons and oil pastels.

Blind Contour Drawings, Gesture Drawings, Cut-Out Contour Collage, Imaginary Drawings (see Figures 52 & 53), Moving Figure Drawings, Group Figure Drawings, Modelled Drawings, Memory Drawings, Observational Drawings, Opposite Hand Drawings, Two-Handed Drawings, Conversation Drawings, *Kitchen Sink Drawings* (the students are asked to include over 20 items in one drawing), *Ghost Drawings* (using a dark pencil and a kneaded eraser, the student draws a series of images on the same page, each time lightly erasing some or all of the image so that a "ghost" remains of the original drawings).

*Figure 52- **Adolescent Art***: Drawing by a 17-year-old teen. Through his involvement with the hip-hop culture, this student became very interested in graffiti art. This drawing uses letters, phrases, and statements to produce an intricate and rhythmic composition. The drawing, which gives us the feeling that it is on the side of a building or a subway car, was signed (or *tagged*) using the artist's street name of "Zen."

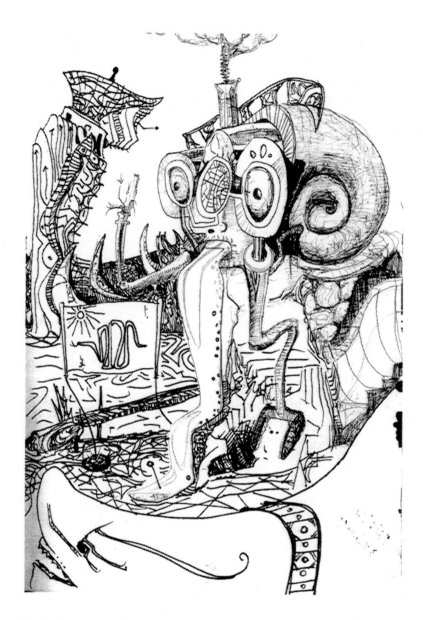

*Figure 53- **Adolescent Art**:* Drawing by a 17-year-old teen. In this inventive and symbolic drawing, the student used amorphous shapes to explore ideas, fantasies, and feelings. Abstract and realistic forms come together to create odd juxtapositions and suggest dreamlike, disassociated images such as machine parts, eyeballs, bending buildings, steps, water, cracked ice, strange creatures, swords, snakes, snails, train tracks, wheels, chimney smoke, and sharks.

Painting—You will need: cardboard, canvas, paper, wood (or whatever surface is available to paint on), water-based paint, paintbrushes, collage materials, found objects, glue, a palette, paper towels or rags.

All of the painting projects from the previous sections would work with this age. Especially relevant and described in Chapter 5 are, from *Schematics:* Self-Portraits with Real or Imaginary Pets, Sequential Story Paintings, Imagine Paintings, and from *Dawning Realists:* Life-Cycle Paintings, Perfect World Paintings, Invention Paintings, and from *Pseudo-Naturalists:* Newspaper Story Paintings, Pop Music Poetry Paintings, Pop Star Paintings and/or Posters (see Figure 54), Lost on an Island Paintings, Pretend Family Paintings, Childhood Memory Paintings, Fly on the Wall Paintings, Doodle/Collage Paintings, and Painting Set-Ups. The following projects are also suggested for adolescents:

*Figure 54 - **Adolescent Art**:* Drawing by a 17-year-old teen. This pop star poster was made by a teen for a local concert that had the theme "Funk Melt Down." By including two people dancing as well as showing all the band members either singing or playing their instruments, he makes us feel like everyone is having a really good time. Notice the piano player's exaggerated hands and the surrealistic way that the piano is melting into the guitar player.

1. *Influential Experience Paintings*—Students are asked to create a painting that describes 6 experiences that have greatly influenced their lives. In order to start the project, students are given a large piece of paper that is divided in half. One-half is blank and the other half is geometrically divided into 6 sections. On the blank half of the paper, the student paints a self-portrait. On the half with the 6 sections, students are asked to use each box to depict 6 different experiences that have affected or possibly changed their lives. Examples of influential experiences may include going through a family crisis, falling in love, learning to play music, breaking up with a girlfriend or a boyfriend, getting into trouble, watching someone you love deal with a serious illness, moving into a new neighborhood, changing schools, or visiting another country.

2. *Slide Projection Paintings*—Slides of 5 contemporary or historical artworks could be projected on the wall. After the works have been discussed, one slide can remain to be used as a backdrop. Students can be asked to create a painting that relates to some aspect of the artwork. For example, if the painting is a still life, the student can use some visual or emotional aspect of it. Examples of visual aspects would be the scale, tones, relationship of objects to one another or the overall space around the shapes. Emotional aspects imply projected feelings, memories, or psychological connections evoked by the images. The idea is not to copy the slide, but to use it as a springboard or catalyst for the creation of an original work of art.

3. *Dada Painting/Collage*—Through slides, photos, books, museums, or the Internet, students can learn about Dada and look at the work of artists such as Marcel Duchamp, Sophie Taeuber-Arp, Kurt Schwitters, and Hannah Höch. (Dada was an avant-garde and antisocial art movement that developed in the early 1900s. By looking at common objects in a new way and taking them out of context, artists challenged everyday assumptions about "reality.") Because of its anarchistic attitude and its emphasis on the absurd, adolescents really connect to it. In the spirit of Dada, students will be asked to create multimedia collages and other structures from found objects and paint.

4. *Improvisational Music Paintings*—To present a more multi-arts approach, a live music session might be arranged where students could attend a concert or have a musician play in the classroom. The class can be asked to create abstract interpretations of the music (pictures of memories or fantasies that the music evokes), or they can be asked to draw the musicians. If it is not possible to have live music in class, then instrumental music tapes such as jazz or classical can be played during the art session. Students are encouraged to create work in any media as long as it represents their own unique response to the music.

5. *Word Association Paintings*—Students are given a piece of paper that has been divided into four sections. They are asked to choose 4 out of the following list of words that describe the way any of us could feel on a given day: *happy, sad, depressed, embarrassed, distracted, excited, confused, surprised, lonely, sick, dreamy, worried, scared, or angry.* In each of the squares, the student is asked to create a painting of the word without using the word itself. To make the project more fun, students should not tell anyone else what their words are. After the paintings are done, the class can try to link the visual images to the words.

6. *Identity Paintings*—This project addresses the question of "Who am I?" by exploring the multiplicity of roles that we all play in society. Students get a piece of paper geometrically divided into 6 sections. In each of the sections, they are asked to paint themselves in some of the various roles that they take on every day. Most of us don't really think about it, but we often become different people at different times, depending on the circumstances. For instance, some of the roles that the adolescent might play could be a big sister or a younger brother, a girlfriend or a boyfriend, a babysitter, a musician and/or a singer in a rock band, a skier, a skateboarder, a baseball player, a tutor, a dancer, or a salesperson working after school in a clothing store. This project heightens awareness about the many facets of our lives and looks at the complex nature of identity.

7. *Surrealist Paintings*—Through slides, photos, books, museums, or the Internet, students are introduced to surrealist artists such as Frida Kahlo, Méret Oppenheim, René Magritte, and Salvador Dalí. (Surrealism was an art movement that overlapped with Dada in the 1920s. Originally a literary movement, it explored dreams, the unconscious, the element of chance, and multiple levels of reality.) Students will look at and discuss incongruous images in surrealist art such as: buildings turned sideways, people gliding through the air, floating rocks, fur-lined tea cups, and melting clocks. Students will be asked to create a series of painting/collages that:

(a) *Change the normal scale of objects*—For example: fruit the size of a living room or bugs that are bigger than people (see Figure 55).

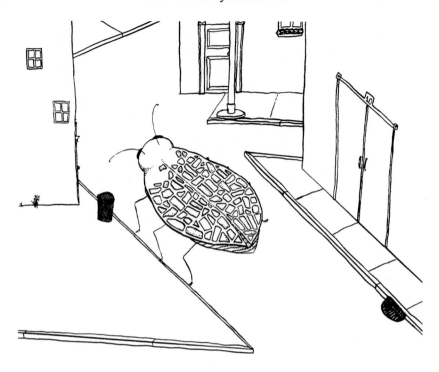

*Figure 55- **Adolescent Art***: Drawing by a 16-year-old teen. In this drawing, the scale of objects is radically changed by having a huge bug walk down an empty street. The bug looks about the size of a large bus or truck. There are no people around, giving the feeling that it is either the middle of the night (and everyone is sleeping) or it is daytime and everyone is scared of the bug, so they are staying inside. Notice the size of the garbage can in relationship to the bug and the interesting use of perspective. It feels as if we are looking at this scene from the upper floor window of an apartment building.

   (b) *Turn the accepted order of things upside-down*–For example: cars that ride on the sidewalk while people walk on the streets, or dogs walking people.
   (c) *Mix internal and external space*–For example: seeing the inside and the outside of an object at the same time, clouds that float inside the living room, or trees growing inside the kitchen (see Figure 56).
   (d) *Transform one object into another*–For example: a car turning into a giant fish or an animal turning into a person.

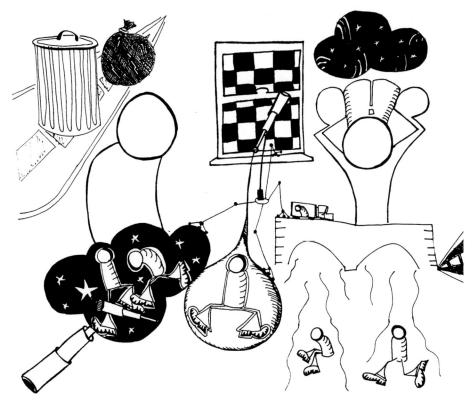

*Figure 56 - **Adolescent Art:*** Drawing by a 16-year-old teen. In this surreal drawing, "inside" and "outside" space are inseparable. Faceless people look through binoculars at clouds that have stars inside of them. The trash could be on a street, inside a house, or just an image in someone's mind. The window is covered with bricks and little people with big feet are running around somewhere, inside clouds and bubbles.

8. *Artists' Presentations*–If possible, teachers can arrange to have practicing artists come into the classroom where they can give a talk and a slide presentation of their work. Alternatively, small groups of students can be taken to studios of local artists to see their work up close. Students should be encouraged to ask the artist whatever questions they want.

Media Deconstruction Collage–You will need: scraps from popular magazines, paint, glue, self-stick labels, paintbrushes, a masonite board or any other surface that can be used for collage.

The following two collage projects look at issues of ethnicity, power, class and gender that are blatantly or subtly implied in everyday media images. Students can choose to work on one or both of these projects:

A. *Ethnicity and Culture Collage:* The point of this project is to critically examine our consumer culture with the goal of decoding some of the messages that we get every day through advertising, TV, and the movies. Specifically, students will look at the way the media portrays ethnic and social class stereotypes. Questions we can ask are, "What kinds of themes about race, status, and power are being played out in advertising? How do media images affect the way we think about ourselves and even the way we act?" Have students view the work of artists such as Carrie Mae Weems and Adrian Piper (both of whom deal with racial identity), Barbara Kruger (who explores advertising and media messages), and Andy Warhol (who turned consumer products such as Campbell's soup cans into icons). Ask students to make a collage out of pop culture magazine scraps collected over a period of weeks and kept in a box for the class to share. Students can put self-stick labels over the images to express what they believe the images are really saying and/or to tell us how the images make them feel.

B. *Gender Collage:* Give students boards that are divided equally in half. Ask them to cut out pictures from popular culture magazines that portray men and women as "models" for the culture. The women can be pasted on one side of the board and the men can be pasted on the other side. The idea is to see what kind of generalizations we can make about the way that the media represents gender. This collage raises many questions about standards of beauty and gender expectations that are implicit in the pictures. Have students view the work of artists such as Frida Kahlo and David Hockney whose figurative work sometimes has androgynous overtones. Interesting class discussions can be generated about this topic and also other social issues reflected by the media (see Figure 57).

*Figure 57 - **Adolescent Art**:* Gender Collage by a 14-year-old teen. This student cut out pop culture figures of men and women (from music magazines) and pasted them on two halves of a large board. She put men on the right side of the board and women on the left. Real CDs were also included in the collage to symbolize the importance of music in connecting fashion with standards of what is considered current and "cool." In talking about this piece, the student said that she thought that the media portrayed men in a more honest way, allowing for imperfections, while women were made to look like glamorized little girls, movie stars, or princesses.

Linoleum Collage—You will need: linoleum prints, glue, and cardboard.

Refer to Chapter 5 under *Dawning Realists* for instructions on how to make linoleum prints. The student makes multiples (about 8 prints) from the original linoleum plate. If she wishes to, the student can change the color each time she prints so that the original image is the same but each repetition is slightly different. After the prints are done, they should be left to dry before being glued together, with no space between them, on a sturdy piece of cardboard.

Mixed Print Collage–You will need: any kind of finished prints, glue, and cardboard.

A collage can be made from a series of finished prints or a combination of scrap prints that the student doesn't mind transforming into something else. The prints should be cut up into the same geometric size (for instance, 4" x 4" pieces). The 4" x 4" squares should be pasted next to each other on a heavy piece of cardboard. Make a few rows and use a couple of prints in each row.

Other Projects to Try: From Preschematics–Vegetable/Found Object Prints, Clay, Mixed Paper Collage, Crayon/Watercolor Resist, Found Object Box Sculptures; from Schematics–Fabric-Painting Collage, (any or all) Painting Projects, Mood Box Sculptures, Clay, String Prints, Glue Prints, Styrofoam Prints, Papier Maché Standing Sculptures, Outdoor Drawing Excursions; from Dawning Realists– Linoleum Prints, Collage Prints, Monotypes, String-Print Box Sculptures, (any or all) Painting Projects, Hanging Papier Maché Sculptures, Self-Portrait/Memory Box Sculptures, Plasticine, Blind Contour Creatures; from Pseudo-Naturalists–(any or all) Painting Projects, 20th Century Artifact Construction, Television Sculptures, Ripped-up Photocopy Collage.

Other Suggestions: Ceramics, art history, fiber art, collage, installation art, painting, printmaking, calligraphy, mixed media, sculpture, jewelry making, papermaking, film/video, graphic design, computer workshops, woodworking, and life drawing may be available for older teens through some university programs, art schools, museums, arts camps, adult education classes, and private studio settings. Also, art school catalogues and arts magazines may advertise for artist apprenticeships or part-time art assistant jobs.

Art References for Adolescents–Art movements to explore: Abstract Expressionism, Color-Field Painting, Conceptual Art, Cubism, Dada, Earth Art, Expressionism, Feminist Art, Graffiti Art, Impressionism, Minimalism, Photorealism, Pop Art, Surrealism. Artists of interest might include:

16th-17th century: Sofonisba Anguissola (1532-1625), Leonardo da Vinci (1452-1519), El Greco (1541-1614), Lavinia Fontana (1552-1614), Michelangelo (1475-1564), Rembrandt (1606-1669), Caterina van Hemessen (1527-1566), Jan Vermeer (1632-1675).

18th century: François Boucher (1703-1770), Angelica Kauffmann (1741-1807), Marie-Louise-Elisabeth Vigée-Librun (1755-1842).

19th century: Paul Gauguin (1848-1903), Eva Gonzalés (1849-1883), Paula Modersohn-Becker (1876-1907), Berthe Morisot (1841-1895), Henry Ossawa Tanner (1859-1937), Vincent van Gogh (1853-1890).

Early-mid 20th century: Joseph Cornell (1903-1973), Salvador Dalí (1904-1989), Sonia Terk Delaunay (1885-1979), Marcel Duchamp (1887-1968), Alberto Giacometti (1901-1966), Arshile Gorky (1904-1948), Hannah Höch (1889-1978), William H. Johnson (1901-1970), Frida Kahlo (1910-1954), Käthe Kollwitz (1867-1945), René Magritte (1898-1967), Henri Matisse (1869-1954), Edvard Munch (1863-1944), Gabriele Münter (1877-1962), Alice Neel (1900-1984), Louise Nevelson (1899-1988), Georgia O'Keeffe (1887-1986), Méret Oppenheim (1913-1985), Pablo Picasso (1881-1973), Jackson Pollock (1912-1956), Mark Rothko (1903-1970), Kurt Schwitters (1887-1948), Alma Thomas (1891-1978).

Mid-late 20th century: Alice Aycock (b.1946), Jean-Michel Basquiat (1960-1988), Romare Bearden (1911-1988), John Biggers (b.1924), Lee Bontecou (b.1931), Louise Bourgeois (b.1911), Christo (b.1935) and Jeanne-Claude (b.1935), Willem De Kooning (1904-1997), Richard Diebenkorn (1922-1993), Audrey Flack (b.1931), Mary Frank (b.1933), Helen Frankenthaler (b.1928), Andy Goldsworthy (b.1956), Ann Hamilton (b. 1956), Duane Hanson (1925-1996), Keith Haring (1958-1990), Eva Hesse (1936-1970), Nancy Holt (b.1938), Jasper Johns (b.1930), Lois Mailou Jones (b.1905), Ed Kienholz (1927-1994), Ana Mendieta (1948-1985), Joan Mitchell (1926-1992), Elizabeth Murray (b.1940), Claes Oldenburg (b.1929), Yoko Ono (b.1933), Howardena Pindell (b.1943), Adrian Piper (b.1948), Katherine Porter (b.1941), Robert Rauschenberg (b.1925), Faith Ringgold (b.1930), Betye Saar (b.1926), Raymond Saunders (b.1934), Sandy Skoglund (b.1946), Kiki Smith (b.1954), Robert Smithson (1938-1973), Nancy Spero (b.1926), Frank Stella (b.1936), Andy Warhol (1928-1987), Carrie Mae Weems (b.1953), Rachel Whiteread (b.1963).

CONCLUSION

Working on this book has given me the opportunity to reflect on my experiences with students and to think more expansively about the crucial role that art can play in the lives of children and adolescents. The experiences I gained while working as an art therapist in mental health centers contributed to my belief in the power of art to build self-esteem and, at its very best, to heal and transform. Working with urban adolescents from conflict-ridden environments had a powerful effect on me. The adolescents with whom I worked were alienated from their families, schools, culture, and, most sadly, from themselves. Although most of them had no memory of ever making art when they were younger, many were able to use it easily as a way to uncover their true feelings and past traumas. The following incident stands out as an example of the transformational powers that art can have, if only for transitional periods of time.

I was working with three adolescents in the art room. A roll of brown wrapping paper had been placed on the floor so that the students could work together on a group mural. The door opened and I looked up to find another student looking down at us. He was not scheduled for the class and seemed to be wandering around the hallway aimlessly. From his body language, I could tell that he was in a hostile mood. I was just about to ask him what was going on when he disappeared around the corner. But within minutes, he came charging down the hallway and burst right back into the art room. Making a mad dash for our paper palette (filled with gooey red, turquoise, and black paint), he grabbed a paintbrush. Before I could say, "Hey, what are you doing?" he started painting the bottom of his shoe. He then stepped directly on a blank part of the brown paper. Looking really satisfied, he said, "How do you like that?" I looked at the paper and saw a very interesting patterned design (from the bottom of his sneaker). I said, "It's great. Can you make another one?" He looked at me in total shock. Surely he assumed I would be really mad. He probably thought (or hoped) that he had ruined our painting. But, neither was true. I encouraged him to contribute to the mural by using his own shoe print as a matrix for other images yet to evolve. He surprised me by spending the next forty-five minutes quietly making more shoe prints and then turning them into sharks, monsters, skeletons, and other inventive creatures. Eventually the mural ended up hanging in the lobby of the school and he received a lot of recognition for his contribution.

Sometime later, in thinking about the incident, I started wondering how a street-toughened teen (who told me that he "never made art") ended up on the floor of the art room, painting, "playing," and exploring art materials with the same enthusiasm as a four-year-old child. Where did it all come from? I realized that, even though he didn't see himself as someone who could make art, the universal impulse to create it was still there. (If it hadn't been, the situation in the art room would have turned out very differently.)

In the process of thinking further about this issue, I came across the work of Hans Prinzhorn who was a German psychiatrist, art historian, and collector of drawings done by mentally ill patients. In 1922, he produced a striking and influential book of his controversial collection. (The book has since been reprinted as *Artistry of the Mentally Ill*.) Not only did Prinzhorn regard these drawings as serious art, but he also believed that the work of the mentally ill threw light on the creative process itself. He was convinced that visual creativity was an undeniable trait in all of us from childhood onwards. Among the many artists who agreed with him was the renowned French artist, Jean Dubuffet. Dubuffet felt strongly that the art in Prinzhorn's collection represented art of the subconscious. He also believed that pure intuitive art expression was not only found among young children and the mentally ill but was also apparent in the work of visionaries, extreme eccentrics, and other "outsiders." But why? The one factor that pulls these groups together is that they are not linked into conformist attitudes and social conventions that can stultify free art expression.

As parents, teachers, and other child-oriented professionals, we should not translate "conformist attitudes" into standardized and rigid ways of thinking about and teaching children's art. In this book, I have introduced the stages of artistic development (originally conceived by Lowenfeld and Brittain) and provided ideas for art projects that are appropriate for each of the stages. But, more important than knowledge of the stages of artistic development or "appropriate" art projects, is providing a nurturing and supportive environment where cognitive growth and creative exploration can unfold. Children need stimulating opportunities where they can develop strong or potentially passionate interests. They have a lot to teach us about seeing the world and about making art. Sometimes we are too caught up with the toils of daily living to look carefully at their artwork and pay close attention to what they are saying.

One of the most important challenges we have today as parents and teachers is keeping the creative spirit alive in children who are growing up in a world that is becoming increasingly homogeneous. Technological advances, pop culture, media influences, and the proliferation of multinational corporations (aided by the power of advertising) have moved young people toward a kind of unprecedented "sameness." Never before could we travel across the world and see people who look and act like one another, dressing in the same outfits, eating the same foods, and listening to the same music. Video games, TV, movies, Internet accessibility, and even children's toys are contributing to a singular, uniform global culture.

Visual art and other forms of sustained creative expression are not only the antithesis of conformity, they are also crucial elements in the evolution of the child's overall development and individuation. Art offers a window into the soul and is also a chronicle of the child's life experiences. When children are very young, they use art to show us how much they are learning, how they feel about things, and what is important to them. When they get older, they use it as a way to reflect on the culture and explore self-identity. As the world becomes more and more alike, it seems even more important for us to try to help children and adolescents keep making art as a crucial way to keep them connected to their uniqueness.

APPENDIX

ART MATERIALS AND SAFETY INFORMATION

Selecting safe art materials is not an option when working with children, it is a *necessity*, especially with children who are chronically ill or hypoallergenic. Children who are asthmatic or have respiratory or immune deficiency conditions may be at increased risk from exposure to harmful chemicals. When choosing art materials, parents and teachers need to know that adult art materials are exempt from consumer paint lead laws. In addition to lead, adult art materials are also allowed to contain many other toxic substances.

To provide adequate warnings, there is a special art materials labeling law in the United States. But, because some of the label terminology can be confusing to consumers, the following explanations, courtesy of art product safety expert, Monona Rossol, may help you decide what to buy:

1. *Conforms to ASTM D-4236.* This statement means that a Board Certified Toxicologist has reviewed the formula in accordance with the toxic labeling standard of the American Society of Testing and Materials (ASTM) and she/he certifies that the label information provides adequate information for safe use.

2. *Hazard statements.* These statements inform users of the kind of harm the product might cause. Examples of hazard statements include "May be harmful by breathing dusts," "Cancer Agent," or " Exposure may cause allergic reactions."

3. *Precautionary statements.* These statements tell the user what actions they must take in order to use the product safely. Examples include: "Keep out of the reach of children," "Wash hands immediately after use," or "Avoid breathing dusts."

4. *Product seals.* These are not necessary, but they identify the company or organization whose toxicologist certified the product. For example, the largest U.S. certifier is the Arts and Creative Materials Institute (ACMI) which issues the AP, CP, and Health Label seals.

5. *The word "nontoxic."* This word does not always mean that the product is completely safe for children. It only means that *if the product is used as the label directs*, it should be safe. For example, art materials such as tempera paints and felt-tip markers are marketed for children and labeled "nontoxic." But, if they are used for face painting, they are no longer considered safe.

155

Rules for choosing products for children:

1. Make sure the ASTM D-4236 conformance statement is on the label.

2. Make sure the product is clearly marketed for children (not adults).

3. Look for hazard statements. There should be none on products for children in grade six and under.

4. Look for precautionary statements. There should be none on products for children in grade six and under.

5. Look for the word "nontoxic" which should be somewhere on the product.

Products to avoid: Solvents and solvent-containing products, sprays, and powdered materials. In general, products that create fumes, get in the air as a spray or a powder, have warnings on them, or create dust should not be used anywhere near children.

Included are: solvent-containing paints; solvent-containing painting media like paint thinners, varnishes, and shellacs; solvent-containing glues like rubber cement, super-glue, and airplane glue; spray products like spray paint and fixatives; powdered paints or dyes, or dusty products like plaster, dry pastels, and chalks.

Products to use: Art materials marketed for children whose labels say "conforms to ASTM D-4236" and list no warnings.

Included are: water-based tempera paints, finger paints, printing inks, watercolors, gouache, felt-tip markers, watercolor crayons, oil pastels, wax crayons, and glue sticks. Also considered safe under most conditions are standard drawing pencils ranging from hard (light) to soft (dark), charcoal pencils, charcoal sticks, china markers (oil-based pencils), conté crayons, fabric scraps, origami paper, assorted colored papers for collage, white school glue, clay, plasticine, blunt paintbrushes, drawing and painting papers, canvas, sheets of Styrofoam, cardboard, plexiglass, rollers for printmaking, and plain newsprint or black and white newspapers for papier maché.

A good source of additional information on art material safety is *The Artist's Complete Health and Safety Guide* by Monona Rossol.

GLOSSARY

Abstract Expressionism–Developed in the 1940s, Abstract Expressionism is a spontaneous, gestural, and experimental painting style that is rooted in psychic self-expression. Aspects of it include *action painting* (dripping, throwing, and pouring paint) and unconventional use of materials, such as house paint. Abstract Expressionists believe that painting is more about evoking a feeling or a sensation than it is about representing anything. Notable Abstract Expressionists include Jackson Pollock, Lee Krasner, Willem De Kooning, and Joan Mitchell.

Armature–A structure usually made out of wire that forms the skeleton of a sculpture.

Automatic Drawings–Drawings that start out with a spontaneous scribble. The scribble then becomes the impetus for more complex images to evolve.

Blind Contour Drawing–A drawing process that involves focusing on the outline edge of a form. The idea is to look at the object being drawn, not the paper.

Brayer–A roller used to roll ink onto the plate during the process of printmaking.

China Marker–A wax-based pencil that comes in different colors.

Collage–A work of art created by pasting paper or other kinds of materials onto a particular surface. Collage can be integrated with other art forms such as drawing, painting, printing, and sculpture.

Color-Field Painting–Developed in the mid-1950s, Color-Field painting was inspired by Abstract Expressionism (especially the *action painting* style and allover compositions of Jackson Pollock). Artists began using paint in ways that eliminated the distinction between subject and background. Color-Field painting is distinguished by luminous areas of color that don't represent things as much as they conjure up moods and feelings. Working on the floor, rather than an easel, Helen Frankenthaler developed the technique of *stain painting* (pouring paint onto raw canvas and allowing the color to seep in), which influenced the work of other notable artists such as Morris Louis and Kenneth Noland.

Conceptual Art–Developed in the mid-1960s, Conceptual Art evolved because some artists were concerned about the overcommercialization of art. Many of them stopped making art products altogether. They presented their work as ideas, not as objects to be bought and sold. Artists such as Yoko Ono, Mel Bochner, and Joseph Kosuth represented their works as written statements, numerical sequences, dictionary definitions, or painting instructions.

Conté Crayon–A thin firm pastel that comes in neutral colors and also earth tones.

Contour Drawings–Expressive line drawings that outline the edge of a form.

Conversation Drawings–Communal drawings where one person draws something and then gives it to a partner who adds to it. The exercise can go on for a while, with the drawing being passed back and forth, until the two people decide that the visual conversation is over.

Cubism–Developed in the early 1900s, Cubism was influenced by intellectual trends, African art, and the paintings of Paul Cézanne. Cubist artists defined a different way of "seeing" and created an entirely new visual language. Objects were depicted as kaleidoscopic fragments of a whole or as if they were being viewed from many angles at the same time. Pablo Picasso and Georges Braque are credited with being the primary force behind the movement, even sometimes working together in the same studio and making paintings that were practically indistinguishable from one another. Cubism influenced other notable artists such as Lois Mailou Jones, whose paintings explored African imagery. Also, Cubist imagery led the way for artists such as Sonia Terk Delaunay and Piet Mondrian to explore total abstraction.

Cut Out Contour Collages–Expressive line drawings made by using scissors instead of a pencil. After the shapes are cut out, they are pasted on another sheet of paper.

Dada–Developed in the early 1900s, the word "Dada" was chosen as the name of this movement because it stands for any nonsense word like "gaga" or "googoo." Dada was an avant-garde, anarchistic movement that challenged all aspects of society, even questioning the definition of "art." Artists such as Marcel Duchamp, Kurt Schwitters, and Hannah Höch transformed found objects, scraps, junk and/or photographs into art by changing the context in which they are seen. For instance, Duchamp took a urinal out of a bathroom, put it into an art gallery and called it *Fountain*. Kurt Schwitters used paper scraps, old newspapers, and bus tickets to make innovative collages and Hannah Höch cut and pasted photographs together to create original photomontages. Dada artists not only challenged the way we look at the world, they also gave everyday objects new meaning.

Earth Art–Developed in the mid-1960s, Earth Art related to the conceptualist idea that art is more than a commercial product. Artists identified with this movement became interested in creating ephemeral work that interacted with the natural world. Using pure materials such as sand, stone, moss, sticks, and clay, some artists sought to blur the distinction between nature and art. Eventually, some of the artworks got dismantled, collapsed, melted, washed away, or deteriorated into the earth. The best known earthwork is Robert Smithson's *Spiral Jetty* (1970), a spiral road that curved into a lake, and eventually was absorbed into the ecosystem. Another earth artist, Nancy Holt, made enormous concrete architectural structures with tunnels that people could walk through. The terms "Earth Art" and "Environmental Art" are sometimes used interchangeably.

Expressionism–Developed in the late 1800s, Expressionist artists (using recognizable images) stopped trying to depict a cold, objective universe and focused instead on painting their emotional and psychological response to it. Expressionism is known for its vibrant and bold colors and distorted, elongated and exaggerated forms. Among the notable Expressionists are Wassily Kandinsky, Gabriele Münter, and Edvard Munch.

Feminist Art–Developed in the late 1960s, Feminist Art maintains that gender plays a major role in how we see and connect to the world (what is personal is also political). The movement focused on creating artwork out of the experience of being a woman. Ana Mendieta created haunting work that connected the female body and nature. Miriam Schapiro incorporated fabric, paint, needlework, and lace with images of female domesticity. Barbara Kruger made art that looked critically at the cultural domination of women through advertising.

Fishing Line–Thin, strong, and invisible-looking monofilament, originally used for fishing, but also useful for hanging objects.

Gesture Drawings–Quick drawings that capture the action or pose of the figure.

Gouache–A watercolor paint that is opaque rather than transparent.

Graffiti Art–Developed in the mid-1970s, Graffiti Art (originally derived from street graffiti) is done on canvas or paper rather than in public spaces. Influenced by street-wise teenagers who spray-painted New York City subway cars, artists like Keith Haring and Jean-Michel Basquiat (aka "Samo") painted graffiti on billboards, street signs, doorways, garbage cans, busses, and the walls of abandoned buildings. Their work got noticed and soon Graffiti Art became associated with bold and intricate word designs and raw cartoon-like figures that symbolized urban youth culture, alienation, and rebelliousness. Since graffiti in public spaces is illegal, street artists (also called *taggers* or *writers*) sign their work with made-up names or initials.

Ghost Drawings–The student draws a series of images on the same page, using a kneaded eraser to remove some or all of the original. Each time the student draws, the images get partially erased, so that what remains is a "ghost" of the original drawings.

Group Figure Drawings–More than one model poses at the same time.

Imaginary Drawings–Drawings that incorporate dreams, memories, ideas, fantasies, or anything that relies on imagination, not observation.

Impressionism–Developed in the 1860s, Impressionism started with artists who got bored of painting portraits of nobility and historical themes and decided to take their easels outside and study nature instead. Focusing primarily on the visual effects of natural light, Claude Monet and Pierre Auguste Renoir developed the technique of placing marks of pure color side by side where the viewer can blend them optically. Among the greatest Impressionists are Mary Cassatt and Berthe Morisot, both of whom explored the theme of mother and child and portrayed women in domestic settings.

Kinesthetic–Refers to movement.

Kitchen Sink Drawings–Students are asked to include 20 or more objects in one drawing.

Mandala–The Sanskrit word for circle.

Masonite–A stiff, processed-wood board that artists often use as a surface for collage or for painting.

The Creativity Handbook

Media–Materials such as paint, pencils, inks, and charcoal sticks that are used to make art.

Minimalism–Developed in the 1960s, artists who identified with Minimalism were more interested in reducing art to its bare essentials (line, form, color, and space) than in creating representational imagery. Works such as black cubes (sometimes factory-produced in multiples) were meant to be viewed in the context of the space around them. Artists such as Frank Stella made stripe paintings, Agnes Martin created faint pencil grids over monochromatic paintings, Anne Truitt made sculptures out of one or two large wooden rectangles, and Dan Flavin made stark environments out of store-bought fluorescent tubes.

Mixed Media–The combined use of different kinds of art materials.

Modelled Drawings–Drawings that focus on light and dark tones of the form such as shadows and folds.

Moving Figure Drawings–The model slowly moves as the student tries to capture some element of the movement.

Memory Drawings–The student draws from memory as opposed to from visual observation.

Monotype–A one-of-a-kind print.

Naturalistic–The attempt to represent subject matter objectively.

Observational Drawings–Drawings that use observation as a starting point for a range of visual interpretations.

Opposite Hand Drawings–Drawings that challenge the students to draw with the opposite hand from the one that they are used to.

Palette–A flat surface used for the purpose of mixing paint. Some examples are wax paper, tinfoil, paper palette (sold in art stores), plexiglass, glass, or an old muffin tin.

Papier Maché–A sticky paper pulp that can be used to build up a surface for creating sculptures and other objects; usually made by dipping strips of newspaper into diluted glue.

Photorealism–Developed in the mid-1960s, Photorealism is a meticulous figurative painting style that uses photos as a take-off point rather than direct observation of the external world. Artists such as Audrey Flack and Chuck Close became interested in how vision is altered by the camera and, more metaphorically, where reality and illusion intersect. Many Photorealists were as much (if not more) involved with photographic effects than they were with their subjects.

Plasticine–An oily clay that never dries.

Plate–The surface that a print is taken from. A plate can be made of plexiglass, wood, metal, cardboard, canvas, or other kinds of material.

Play Dough–A nonpermanent, malleable, clay-like material (either made at home or bought in a store) that children can mold easily.

Pop Art–Developed in the early 1960s, Pop Art had to do with turning banal images of mass culture into monumental icons. Influenced by advertising and commercialism, artists painted coke bottles, food, household appliances and other utilitarian objects in a nonemotional, slick, and representational painting style. Andy Warhol is best known for creating multiple images of Campbell soup cans. Roy

Lichtenstein painted enlarged frames from comic strips and Claes Oldenburg made soft sculptures of everyday items such as hamburgers and telephones. Few women artists were involved in the movement, possibly because consumer culture was depicted primarily from a male perspective.

Public Art–Developed in the late 1960s, Public Art is made for and owned by the community (an ancient concept going way back to cave paintings, frescoes, and commemorative statues). Public Art was a natural outgrowth of Earth Art, where artists started making artwork that interacted with the environment. In a climate of expansive ideas that were redefining "art," some artists began viewing their work as a part of the public arena rather than as a private commodity. This change in thinking converged with government initiatives to support art in public spaces. Examples of public artworks are Christo's and Jeanne-Claude's wrapped buildings, Alexander Calder's stabiles, Maya Lin's Vietnam War Memorial, Joyce Kozloff's tiled murals in subway stations, and Judy Baca's murals of the history of Los Angeles and its Hispanic communities.

Scale–The size of an object.

Schema–Simple, geometric forms that represent the child's active knowledge of a subject. After about the age of 7, the child develops schemas that she repeats and refines until she is emotionally and developmentally ready to let them go.

Surrealism–Developed in the 1920s, and influenced by Freud, Surrealism was a direct outgrowth of Dada. Originally a literary movement, it explored dreams, the unconscious, the element of chance, and multiple levels of reality. Putting familiar objects in odd juxtapositions, artists like Salvador Dalí and René Magritte created hallucinatory images such as melting clocks, gigantic rocks floating in midair, and indoor clouds. Frida Kahlo made paintings that combined internal and external space, dream images, historical and autobiographical references, and symbols. Méret Oppenheim became known for transforming everyday objects into mysterious works of art. Her fur-lined tea cup, saucer and spoon, exhibited in 1937 (once considered shocking), is now one of the most celebrated and recognized symbols of the movement.

Tone–Refers to color or hue.

Two-Handed Drawings–Drawings made with two hands at the same time, sometimes using different materials in each hand.

Visual Language–Nonverbal communication created through visual images instead of words.

Visual Thinking–Perceiving and thinking about the world using mental images.

BIBLIOGRAPHY

Amabile, Teresa M. *Creativity in Context.* Westview Press, Inc., Boulder, CO, 1996.

Amabile, Teresa M. *The Social Psychology of Creativity.* Springer-Verlag, New York, 1983, p.15.

Archer, Michael. *Art Since 1960.* Thames and Hudson, Ltd., London, 1997.

Arnheim, Rudolf. *Visual Thinking.* University of California Press, Berkeley, CA, 1969.

Atkins, Robert. *Art Speak.* Abbeville Press, New York, 1997.

Burton, Judith M. "Representing Experiences: Ideas in Search of Forms." *SchoolArts.* Davis Publications, Inc., January, 1981: 58-64.

Carlsson-Paige, Nancy & Diane E. Levin. *Who's Calling the Shots?* New Society Publishers, Philadelphia, 1990.

Csikszentmihalyi, Mihaly. *Creativity.* HarperCollins, New York, 1996.

Csikszentmihalyi, Mihaly, Kevin Rathunde, & Samuel Whalen. *Talented Teenagers.* Cambridge University Press, New York, 1993, p.26.

Edwards, Betty. *Drawing on the Right Side of the Brain.* J.P. Tarcher, Inc., Los Angeles, 1979.

Erikson, Erik. H. *Identity: Youth and Crisis.* W.W. Norton and Company, New York, 1994, p.163.

Fineberg, Jonathan. *The Innocent Eye: Children's Art and the Modern Artist.* Princeton University Press, Princeton, NJ, 1997.

Gardner, Howard. *Art, Mind and Brain.* Basic Books, New York, 1982.

Gardner, Howard. *Artful Scribbles.* Basic Books, New York, 1980.

Goleman, Daniel, Paul Kaufman, & Michael Ray. *The Creative Spirit.* Penguin Books, New York, 1993.

Heller, Nancy G. *Women Artists.* Abbeville Press, New York, 1997.

Kaupelis, Robert. *Experimental Drawing.* Watson-Guptill Publications, New York, 1980.

Kaupelis, Robert. *Learning to Draw.* Watson-Guptill Publications, New York, 1983.

Kellogg, Rhoda. *Analyzing Children's Art.* Mayfield Publishing, Mountain View, CA, 1970.

Kellogg, Rhoda. *What Children Scribble and Why.* N-P Publications, Palo Alto, CA, 1959.

Levick, Myra. *See What I'm Saying.* Islewest Publishing, Dubuque, IA, 1998.

Lowenfeld, Viktor & W. Lambert Brittain. *Creative and Mental Growth.* Macmillan, New York, 1987.

Maizels, John. *Raw Creation: Outsider Art and Beyond.* Phaidon Press, London, 1996.

Powell, Richard J. *Black Art and Culture in the 20th Century.* Thames and Hudson, Ltd., London, 1997.

Read, Herbert. *A Concise History of Modern Painting.* Thames and Hudson, Ltd., London, 1985.

Robinson, Walter. *Instant Art History.* Fawcett Columbine, New York, 1995.

Rosen, Randy & Catherine C. Brawer. *Making Their Mark: Women Artists Move into the Mainstream, 1970-85.* Abbeville Press, New York, 1989.

Rossol, Monona. *The Artist's Complete Health and Safety Guide.* Allworth Press, New York, 1994.

Schirrmacher, Robert. *Art and Creative Development for Young Children.* Delmar Publishers, Albany, NY, 1998.

Silberstein-Storfer, Muriel & Mablen Jones. *Doing Art Together.* Simon and Schuster, New York, 1982.

Singer, Dorothy G. & Tracey A. Revenson. *A Piaget Primer.* Penguin Group, New York, 1996.

Walsh, Michael. *Graffito.* North Atlantic Books, Berkeley, CA, 1996.

INDEX